# THE LONDON BLITZ

# THE LONDON BLITZ

## The City Ablaze, December 29, 1940

David Johnson

STEIN AND DAY/*Publishers*/New York

*J M*

Published in the United States of America in 1981.
Copyright © 1980 by David Johnson

All rights reserved.
Printed in the United States of America
Stein and Day/*Publishers*/Scarborough House, Briarcliff Manor, N.Y. 10510

*Library of Congress Cataloging in Publication Data*

Johnson, David, 1950–
    The London blitz.

    Originally published: The city ablaze.—London:
W. Kimber, 1980.
    Includes index.
    1. London (England)—Bombardment, 1940. I. Ti-
tle.

| D760.8.L7J63 1981 | 940.54 ′21 | 80-6199 |
| ISBN 0-8128-2799-6 | | AACR2 |

# Contents

# List of Illustrations

# MAPS

# Acknowledgements

Tracking down the facts about the 29th December Fire Blitz nearly forty years after the event did present its difficulties. Over the years, official files and documents had been lost or misplaced, or sometimes deliberately destroyed. In the data that did turn up, there were often more than a few discrepancies and contradictions. The Luftwaffe archives supplied two different sets of take-off times and two completely different total numbers of attacking aircraft, both of which were enclosed in the same envelope. Some aspects had to be made up from hundreds of small bits of information like a glass mosaic, such as the chapters dealing with the X-Beams. Other segments were pieced together from material that was almost non-existent.

These shortcomings were balanced by the co-operation of those people mentioned in the Acknowledgements, who were so generous with their time and efforts. Without their assistance, researching this book would have been next to impossible.

First, I should like to thank the following newspapers for their support and co-operation; quite simply, without them there would have been no book,

*UK PRESS Gazette*
*City Recorder*
*Evening News*
*Daily Mirror*, especially Peter Reed, the Letters' Editor.

A number of City firms also went out of their way to help me in my quest for information, and for photographs:

Lloyds Bank, and the Bank of England, and the editors of their company magazines *The Dark Horse* and *The Old Lady*, were helpful in gathering a few eye-witnesses of the air raid.

I would like to thank Anthony O. Akers of Baring Brothers & Co. Ltd, for his help.

I should like to express my gratitude to Eric Stratford, of C.E. Heath & Co, Ltd, for his efforts.

Mr. C. Williams, of Hitchcock, Williams & Co. Ltd, deserves a vote of thanks for allowing me to interview two employees during company time.

Mr. T.W. Syrett, Hon Secretary of the 'Round Threads', the London Fire Brigade Retired Members Association, supplied me with the names and whereabouts of a number of firemen and Brigade Officers who were in the City on 29th/30th December 1940.

The London Fire Brigade's Librarian, Mr James O'Sullivan, also gave me some important information. The Photographic Branch was also of great assistance.

Excerpts from the Fire Squad's Reports at Guildhall appear by courtesy of the Corporation of London; the source of these documents is the Corporation of London Records Office. I should like to thank Miss Betty R. Masters, Deputy Keeper of the Records, for her assistance in suggesting the documents in the first place, and also for seeking out the names and whereabouts of the parties involved in the fires.

At St. Paul's Cathedral, Mr Harvey, the Clerk of Works, and Mr A.R.B. Fuller, the Librarian, rendered invaluable help by allowing me to wander about under their guidance, and by answering my questions.

The archivists at both Guy's Hospital, Southwark, and St Bartholomew's Hospital, Smithfield, were both very kind to allow access to hospital records and reports pertaining to 29th/30th December.

I owe a special debt of thanks to the Imperial War Museum. Without the peace and quiet of its reading room, I probably would never have got any work done at all. The entire staff was enormously helpful, but I would like to single out Mr George Clout for his assistance. Mr Clout patiently answered all of my many nagging and persistent questions, and managed to come up with a few suggestions of his own, before I had time to ask about them.

I would like to thank the Militarchiv section of the Bundesarchiv in Freiburg for their help in providing information on the Luftwaffe's participation in the raid.

I would like to thank the Columbia Broadcasting System, New York, for allowing me to quote from Edward R. Murrow's broadcast from 29th December, and the Milo Ryan Phonoarchives in Seattle, Washington, for their assistance with the Murrow broadcasts.

Lastly, I owe a lot to the contributors, listed separately, for their time and efforts in relating their own stories of the night of 29th December, and the morning of 30th December 1940.

Last, but not least, I would like to register a debt of gratitude to Marg Innes for her help with letters and photographs.

# List of Contributors

This book is the combined efforts of City residents, as well as people living throughout London and the neighbouring counties; employees of City firms; and members of the London Fire Brigade. Each name is followed by the eye-witness's vantage point. For members of the Fire Brigade, station, rank, and branch of the Fire Service (either regular LFB or Auxiliary Fire Service) is given.

Anthony O. Akers: Bishopsgate
Connie Aldridge: Chiswell Street
L.P. Andrews: ARP (Air Raid Precautions)
              Emergency Fire Boats, Tilbury, Essex
S.E. Arthur: Oxford Circus Underground Station
Leonard Atkinson: Ludgate Hill

Mark Baring: Bishopsgate
J.W. Barker: A F S, West Hampstead
V.J. Barnes: City
Olive Bayliss (now Mrs Olive Blakey): London Wall
Janet Beeston: in transit
Thomas Bell: Sub-Officer, L F B.; Guy's Hospital
Geoffrey Blackstone: L F B; Guy's Hospital
A.T. Berkshire: A F S Barbican Area
L.E. Benning: in transit
Sally Bourns: Fore Street
Mr and Mrs Ernest Boyd: Sydenham and City
Mrs Marjorie Brinkman: in transit
Mrs E.M. Brooker: Threadneedle Street
Mrs D Bugden

Ivy Cailes: City
W. Callaghan: A F S, Manchester Square
Ateo Cassadio: A R P City
Charlotte Chaddock: Moorgate
Stanley G. Champion: Old Street
J.R. Chick: Liverpool Street Station
Mrs Violet Clarke: Mansion House Underground Station
Juliette M. Clayton
Mrs Emily Clompton: Holborn Viaduct
Mrs L Collier: Rotherhithe
Mrs D. Collings: Faraday Building
R.C.H. Constable: Fore Street
D. Cook: Lloyds Bank
E.R. Cooke: Hornsey
Mrs A. Cordery: Lloyds Bank
R.E. Crowfoot: City of London Police Reserve

Mrs Eileen Dale: Streatham, City
Benjamin W. Davis: Dowgate Dock
Edward Davis: A F S
H. Davis: City
Yvonne Devall
Mrs Joanne Douglas: Regent Street and Streatham

Ian Eaton: Old Street
Arthur Edwards: City of London Police Reserve

Miss M. Ferriter: Farringdon Road
Leslie I. Finegold: Fleet Street
Mrs Phyllis Fisher: Chelsea
H.T. Freeman: Custom Street, E 16

George Garwood: St. Paul's Cathedral
Mrs E. Gifford: St. John Street, Islington
James Goldsmith: L F B, Redcross Street Station
Mr & Mrs A.W.F. Grafton: East Ham and City
Mrs Gladys Greenwood
Mrs Winnifred Grubb: in transit

Joy Hadfield: Southwark and St Paul's Churchyard
G.R. Hagon: A F S Bermondsey Street, Southwark
Trudy Hannington: City
Dorothy Harms: City Road, and City
Mrs Frances Hine: Isleworth, Middlesex
Alfred Hobdell: Broad Street Station
Richard B. Horne: Sub Officer, LFB, Wandsworth
T.R. Hower: Blackfriars
Richard Howlett: City of London Civil Defence
Reginald Huggins: St Paul's Churchyard
Patricia Hutchings: Grocers' Hall
Mr and Mrs John Hyman: Shoreditch
Kenneth N. Hoare: Assistant Divisional Officer, Northern
                Division, L F B, Euston Fire Station

Mrs Ivy Ing: Lime Street
Margaret Ingram: Clapham

Lilian Jack (now Mrs Lilian Vern-Smith): Cripplegate
Doreen Jarvis: City
John W. Jenner: Metropolitan Police, Southwark
A.Y. Jessiman: Ludgate Hill
Mrs Dorothy Johnson: Waterloo Station
H.W. Johnson: East Acton
Ronald Joyce: Paddington

Edward Kelcey: A F S Barnes
Gordon Ketchen: Sidcup, Kent
Kathleen King: Gresham Street

Frank Lawrence: Sub-Officer, L F B Headquarters, Lambeth,
                and Guildhall
F.R. Levander: Bank of England
Joseph Levinter: Whitecross Street
A.G. Lewin: Gidea Park, Essex, and Goswell Rd.

James Mayes: A F S, Ambler School Station, Finsbury Park
Mrs Eileen McConville: Waterloo Station

Mrs D Meadowcroft:
E. Geoffrey Mosely: A F S Hendon
J.A. Mulvany: Bank of England
Frank W. Munson: Guildhall
John W. Murphy: Guildhall

William E. Norwood: Superintendent, L F B Aldersgate St.

Laurence J. Odling: Station Officer, L F B Whitefriars Fire
             Station
Fredrick Offord: Sub Officer, LFB Redcross Street Fire Station

Frank Paling: City
Gordon Papps' St. Paul's Churchyard
Vera Paxton: Croydon, Surrey
Mrs S. Penn: Tower Hill
W. Perrett: A F S
R. Pillow: W R N S, in transit
Mrs M Pledger: Tottenham North

Mrs Rose Rich: London Bridge Station, and Monument Under-
             ground Station
Mrs Olive Rimmell: Chiswell Street
L.C. Roberts: in transit
F. Rogers: Royal Army, Woolwich
Miss A.E. Roos: St. Paul's Churchyard
A. Rosefield: AFS St. Bride's Church, Fleet Street
Philip Rust: Royal Army, London Bridge Station

M.S. Saunders: Exchange Street, and Wenlock Road, Islington
W.W. Seal: Peckham
Eleanor Searle: City
Ray Seels: L F B Islington
Mrs Esther Seymour: City
Mrs Betty Skinner: London Bridge Station
Mrs B.E. Smith: Ironmonger Lane
Mrs C. Smokes: London Bridge Station
Charles Sone: Guildhall, and City

Mrs Edith Stannett: Southwark
Mrs J. Statcher: Bridewell Place
Eric Stratford: Royal Army, Ashford, Mddx.
A.F.S. Sullivan: Senior Staff Officer to Chief of Fire Staff, LFB

H. Thomas: in transit
Leonard Thomas: Faraday Building
Miss E. Thompson: Minories
Marjorie Thyer: Sister at University College Hospital; in transit
Mrs G. Timbers: in transit
Denys Tuckett: Queen Victoria Street
T.R. Tower: Blackfriars

Eileen Walker: City
Mrs M.B. Walker: in transit
Mrs Doris Walsby: Lloyds Bank
Eileen Waterman: Banner Street
Mrs G. White: Upminster, Essex
Mr and Mrs StanleyH. White: Bermondsey
F. Whittle: Engine driver; Waterloo Station
Leslie Williams: A FS Kentish Town
Sid Willmott: Sub-Officer, L F B Barbican area
Constance Wilson: City
Myrtle Wiseman: Bank of England
Mrs E.A. Wood: City, Wormwood Street
Ron Woolaway: Tramcar Incident, Victoria Embankment
Mrs Evelyn Wright: City
Frank Wright: Surgery Attendant, St Bartholomew's Hospital

# CHAPTER ONE

# No Man's Land
## *Morning*

Special Constable R.E. Crowfoot, City of London Police Reserve, was out of bed at 6 a.m. A few minutes later, he left his house and was on his way to Moor Lane Police Station, in the City district near Moorgate Underground Station, where he was scheduled to go on duty at 7 a.m.

Today, 29th December 1940, was Special Constable Crowfoot's birthday, his forty-first. But he would not have the chance to do much celebrating; he was due on parade at 6.50, and had an eight-hour watch to stand afterwards. As he went on duty at 7 o'clock Crowfoot hoped that his birthday would be routine and uneventful, which would at least be some compensation.

This was a special week-end for Dorothy Harms of City Garden Row, Islington, about a mile north of Moor Lane Police Station. Friday had been her fifteenth birthday. Yesterday she had got her first job, working in a shirt factory in the City with her school friend, Florrie. Today was the day before the great event. She was to start work on Monday morning, and couldn't help showing her excitement.

Not many others found anything about the City of London, the old 'square mile', particularly exciting this Sunday. Stretching from the western end of Fleet Street eastward to the Tower of London, and north from the River Thames to London Wall (the name of a street built upon the foundations of the old Roman wall), the City languished in its weekly Sabbath slumber. The jigsaw puzzle of unoccupied office blocks, warehouses, and churches all huddled under the great grey dome of St Paul's Cathedral, which dominated the entire area from atop Ludgate Hill.

The City has a personality and a history all its own, different and apart from the rest of London. This 'square mile' was originally a walled city; the boroughs that make up modern Greater

London grew around it. It was already a community of consider-able importance by the first century AD, when it was called Londinium by the Romans. The Saxon king Alfred the Great made London the capital of his kingdom in the ninth century. The City is still largely self-governed, administered from the ancient Guildhall, the City's 'town hall'. The City of London also has its own police force, distinguished from the regular Metro-politan force by their coxcomb helmets.

Probably more than any other landmark, Guildhall symbolises the entire district. This grandiose-looking brown stone building played an active part in countless events throughout London's past, both great and disastrous. It is a mix of history, sentiment, and work-a-day, the same things that most Londoners see in the old 'square mile'. The current Guildhall dates from 1411 but underwent much alteration in the 1860s, when the outline of the City was also being changed by almost constant construction.

Even though it still maintained the look of a fifteenth-century curiosity piece, with its steeply gabled roof and ornate main entrance, Guildhall was not merely just a quaint old place. The halls and offices of the complex were still the seat of the local government and, since the outbreak of the war, its control centre was a vital link with the City's fire stations and Air Raid Warden's posts. The courts of the City were also held here; this was one of the City's living links with the past. The courts of the Common Council and the Lord Mayor still heard trials, just as they had done in 1553 when Lady Jane Grey, the Queen for Nine Days, had been found guilty of treason against her cousin, Queen Mary I.

Except for its main walls, Guildhall was totally destroyed in the Great Fire of London in September 1666, along with every other building in the vicinity. The fire broke out in a baker's shop in Pudding Lane, in the eastern part of the City near the Tower, on Sunday, 2nd September and, fanned by strong winds, raged across the town for four days and nights. This was not the first time that the City burned, nor would it be the last. The closely-packed buildings and narrow streets allowed fires to spread at will. When the flames finally burned themselves out on 6th September 1666, nearly 90% of the City — over 13,000 houses and 400 streets — had been reduced to piles of ashes.

"The jigsaw puzzle of office blocks, warehouses, and churches . . ." One of the City's few roof spotters scans the southern sky for aircraft. The cramped, narrowly-spaced buildings, clearly evident here, allowed even the smallest fire to spread out with alarming speed.

The Monument, standing in the middle of Monument Street, is a memorial to the Great Fire of 1666. It stands 202 feet high — the exact distance to the shop in Pudding Lane where the Fire began. No monuments have been erected to the City's numerous other fires, however. The worst blaze in recent times had been the great Cripplegate fire of 1897, which acquired almost legendary stature among old-timers in the London Fire Brigade.

The task of rebuilding after the 1666 Fire fell to Christopher Wren, a leading mathematician and architect who had been appointed to the Royal Commission for reconstruction. In 1667, Wren began rebuilding many of the City's 87 parish churches and other buildings that had perished, including the Guildhall. Many of Christopher Wren's churches are famous for their graceful steeples, especially St Bride's Church on Fleet Street, its elegant four-tiered tower lauded as 'a madrigal in stone', and St Mary-le-Bow, said to have the finest spire of all. The rest of the City also emerged from the ruins. New shops sprang up all around, keeping pace with Wren's imagination and energy.

After the 1666 fire, London rapidly expanded even further beyond the walls of the old City. A century later the walls themselves were torn down, but the City's seven gates — Ludgate, Newgate, Cripplegate, Aldersgate, Moorgate, Bishopsgate, and Aldgate — still remain as the names of streets. Recovery from the Great Fire was remarkably swift. By the end of the seventeenth century, the City had resumed its centuries-old role as a centre of commerce and trade.

In 1940 it was still a lively place during the working week. Messengers scooted through narrow alleys to small, out-of-the-way offices. Buses jammed Cheapside, Cannon Street and Queen Victoria Street. Along with the familiar red double-decker buses, there were now also green, blue, brown, and white coaches, sent by cities throughout England to replace the London Transport vehicles destroyed since the Luftwaffe's nighttime bombing raids began on 7th September. Their varied shapes and hues certainly lent a dash of colour to the streets, but also made the traffic congestion seem somehow even more frantic.

The textile and clothing warehouses along Fore Street and Redcross Street, and the book trade in Paternoster Square and

Ave Maria (pronounced by City natives to rhyme with 'wave hi-ya') Lane, did a brisk business. The Bank of England, the Royal Exchange, and Lloyds Bank, over in the East End, made the City the financial heart of Britain. The almost countless streets and lanes in between were lined with shops and offices. On weekdays, and on Saturdays before one o'clock, the streets were hardly wide enough to hold all the traffic.

But on Sunday, they were nearly empty. On Saturday afternoon, businessmen locked their offices and left for home for the rest of the weekend. The City was even more deserted than usual on this weekend. It was the last Sunday of the year. Christmas had just passed, and New Year was only three days away. Everyone who could possibly arrange it had left for the country on Friday, or at least early on Saturday. Every office, factory, and shop was shut; even the pubs were closed. People jokingly called the area a ghost town. Charles Sone, who lived across the river in Southwark, had his own name. He called the empty City 'no man's land'.

In Paris, at the headquarters of Generalfeldmarschall Hugo Sperrle, the commanding general of Luftflotte 3, the atmosphere was anything but quiet. A huge, pulpy man, Hugo Sperrle looked as though he might have been cast for his part as Luftwaffe Feldmarschall by Hollywood: the fleshy red face, the short-cropped hair, the monocle, all combined to give him an unmistakably Teutonic look. He had been practising saturation bombing since the Spanish Civil War in 1936, and, although an expert in the field, was always trying new ways to perfect the technique. Since the night bombing of London had begun early in September, Sperrle had been alternating between the use of heavy high-explosive bombs and the small but lethal incendiary bombs against his target, always looking for a more efficient means of destruction. He did not yet know it, but the Feldmarschall was about to be given another occasion to polish his expertise in mass bombing.

Sometime after breakfast, the telephone rang in Feldmarschall Sperrle's suite in the Hotel Luxembourg, giving the Luftwaffe chief the news that a heavy air raid had been ordered for tonight. The Führer of the German Third Reich, Adolf Hitler, had personally ordered a full-scale air strike to be carried out by Luftflotte 3

— the target: London. Now Sperrle and his aides had a myriad of things to do to prepare for tonight's effort: notifying the bombing groups, choosing the bomb loads, and a score of other details.

The choice of London as tonight's target was no passing whim. Hitler, and his Luftwaffe Commander-in Chief, Hermann Göring, had been waiting over a week for the chance to pay Britain back after the recent bombing attacks against German cities. The heavy raid on Berlin on 20th December was the most humiliating. On this night, the RAF had damaged railway stations, freight yards, docks and factories during several hours of intensive pounding from the air.

Adolf Hitler was enraged by the bombing of the Third Reich's capital city, and Reichsmarschall Göring, who had once boasted that no enemy aircraft would dare to attack the Fatherland, took each bomb as a personal affront. The vulgar, egocentric Göring, famous during the First World War as a fighter pilot, and the last commander of the famous Richthofen Geschwader, regarded the British air raids as so many slaps-in-the-face to his Luftwaffe. A particularly bad raid, like the one against Berlin, also put him in a bad light with Hitler, whom he feared above all men.

Both Hitler and Göring were eager to retaliate against London. But the weather during the past week, calm but very foggy, had shut down all of the Luftwaffe's airfields in northern France. Nothing resembling an all-out attack on the British capital could be mounted, although a light raid had been launched on Friday. Today, however, it look as though the weather would clear, and that the Luftwaffe would get its opportunity.

The Blitz against London, the series of aerial attacks that had begun on Sunday, 7th September 1940, had been triggered by revenge. Up to 7th September, the Luftwaffe's target had been the Royal Air Force. In August, the Battle of Britain had been slowly slipping away from the young Spitfire and Hurricane pilots, as the Luftwaffe's concentrated attacks on the RAF's airfields and communications networks drained Fighter Command of its strength. The RAF had lost more aircraft than the Luftwaffe, despite all claims to the contrary, and more than one quarter of Britain's fighter pilots had been either killed outright or disabled. Disaster was brewing for Britain. Only a few more weeks of such

'...an unmistakably Teutonic look.' Generalfeldmarschall Hugo Sperrle, Commander of *Luftflotte* 3 and planner of the Fire Raid.

losses and the Luftwaffe's mastery of the sky would be absolute. Hitler would be able to invade southern England before the autumn weather turned against him.

On 24th August, the RAF received an unexpected reprieve. On this night, a force of Luftwaffe bombers, searching for the oil tanks at Thamshaven and Purfleet, overflew their target and dropped their bombs on Central London. The following night, Prime Minister Winston Churchill ordered a reprisal raid on Berlin. This, in turn, led to counter-reprisals and a change of tactics by Hitler — London would be subject to massive bombings. On 4th September, Adolf Hitler boasted from Berlin's Sportsplatz, 'If they attack our cities, we shall raze *theirs* to the ground!'

In this, at least, Hitler was as good as his word. Britain's dwindling defensive screen had been spared. On 15th September, the RAF achieved victory over the Luftwaffe, forcing Hitler to make his raids on London under the cover of night. London was bombed every night for fifty-seven nights — from 7th September to 2nd November inclusively. The tone of the bombing war had been established: vengeance — heavy raid for heavy raid.

By December the Luftwaffe's nocturnal visits had become less frequent, and London was enjoying a rest from the attacks. The bombers had come over only twice during the past week: on Sunday, the 22nd, a week ago, and on last Friday, the 27th. Last Sunday's had been a 'light raid' — it didn't even make the front page of the next day's *News Chronicle* — although the House of Lords had been slightly damaged. Other areas throughout England had been bombed on that night as well, most notably the city of Manchester.

The Manchester raid introduced a new tactic by the Luftwaffe: the Fire Blitz. Thousands of foot-long incendiary bombs had been dropped in an intensive night-long attack. The use of incendiary bombs — IBs — was nothing new. They had been dropped frequently throughout the Blitz, usually along with loads of high-explosive bombs, weighing 550 pounds each. But this had been the first time that fire bombs had been dropped exclusively, and in such great quantities.

The Luftwaffe had set out to burn Manchester to the ground, and had largely succeeded. Whole sections of that city blazed out of control for hours last Sunday night. Entire blocks of flats and offices were burnt out, reduced to smouldering wrecks by daybreak. In the morning, people on their way to work looked on as firemen continued to fight the fires.

Ironically, incendiaries were the easiest type of bomb to deal with. There was little that anyone could do about a 550 pound high-explosive bomb except run for cover. But anyone who could use a shovel or drop a sandbag could extinguish an IB.

An incendiary bomb measured about one foot in length, about three inches in diameter, and weighed one kilogramme (2.2 lbs). When a fire bomb landed on a roof or struck the pavement its magnesium core burst into life, throwing a glittering shower of white, molten splinters in a radius of about ten feet. After about a minute it stopped sputtering and began to glow intensely, at about 4,000°F, for roughly ten minutes. After ten minutes, it finally burned itself out. A sandbag or a shovel full of earth would quickly snuff out a glowering incendiary. Once it stopped sputtering, it could be picked up on a spade and disposed of. The only way not to douse one was with water. A 1939 Public Information leaflet exclaimed, *'If you throw a bucket of water on a burning incendiary, it will explode and throw burning fragments in all directions.'*

Station Officer Laurence J. Odling of Whitefriars Fire Station aptly described the IB as 'not a very clever bomb'. Although not the most sophisticated of weapons, its small size was its great advantage. The bombs were packed in cylindrical containers called 'Molotov Breadbaskets', with 36 bombs in each container. One bomber could carry five of these containers — which equals 180 incendiary bombs. After being released, the 'Breadbasket' burst open at a pre-set altitude, spilling its contents over a confined area.

The small, toy-like incendiaries were deceptively innocent looking. Even one could cause serious damage in an alarmingly short time if left unattended.

A resident of the West End recalls having his card game interrupted one night by a determined banging at his front door. Irritated by the disturbance, he got up to give the noisemaker a piece of his mind. He opened the door to have a breathless Air Raid Warden shout in his face that his house was on fire. The resident looked where the Warden was pointing and, sure enough, saw a glow coming from one of the upper-storey windows.

The man ran upstairs, closely followed by the Warden, and found the upper floor filled with smoke. One incendiary was found in the maid's bedroom, and was put out in less than five minutes. But before it had been dealt with, the single two pound bomb had done £100 in damage. If the Warden had not seen the fire in time, the havoc would undoubtedly have been much worse.

Manchester had suffered such extreme damage because the city's fire brigade had not been able to reach most fires while still in the early stages, before they had a chance to take hold. Almost every building that had been destroyed was securely locked for the weekend. When a building was hit by an incendiary, firemen were forced to break down the door to gain entrance, or else look for another door. By the time they were able to enter the damaged building, the fire was usually out of control.

In its editorial page, on the morning of the 29th *The Observer*, the London newspaper, condemned Manchester's lack of preparation, declaring that 'much of the damage caused by fire in Manchester would have been averted by proper precautions'. The column ended with this statement, which would take on an ironic tinge before the day ended: 'One would have thought there was by this time no city in which the importance of the precaution involved could go unrecognised.'

Adolf Hitler and Hermann Göring both received full reports of the Manchester fire raid, as did the commander of Luftflotte 2, Albert Kesselring, in Brussels, and Generalfeldmarschall Hugo Sperrle, at Air Fleet Three Headquarters in Paris. The reports on the unique, full-scale use of incendiary bombs glowed with praise. Because the Manchester raid had been so successful. Sperrle decided that a large-scale incendiary raid would be directed against London the next time an air strike was ordered — what had worked once could well work again. Along with the Manchester accounts, the Luftwaffe chiefs had also been given several other bits of information that would have a profound effect on tonight's planned attack against London.

From the way the weather was looking, it seemed as though the long-awaited vengeance raid might not get the green light after all.

The weather report handed in this morning by the meteorological experts was far from good. The blanket of solid fog and overcast, which had been curtailing flight operations for over a week, had, at first, seemed to be breaking at last. But now it looked as though the heavy clouds might not dissipate after all. The weather men could give no assurances that a full-strength air raid could be launched before the storm front closed in on the French airfields, making operations impossible.

But another report, submitted long before, made it seem imperative that the air strike be launched tonight regardless of weather predictions. This paper had to do with, of all things, variations of the tides. The position of the moon on the 29th would cause abnormally low tides in Western Europe, including the Thames River Valley. Because of the unusually strong pull of the earth's sister planet, the great, broad ribbon of the River Thames would be drained to a small, narrow stream – making it all but useless as a source of water to London's Fire Brigade. The Luftwaffe would not have to worry about London's permanent 'primary water main' – it would have been neutralised before any German aircraft left the ground. If enough serious fires were started in the British capital – especially in the district surrounding St Paul's Cathedral, crammed with old, highly inflammable buildings, as well as more than its share of military targets – the existing water mains could not supply the Fire Brigade with enough water to put them out.

Aside from the low tides, there was another factor that favoured an air strike against London tonight. This detail could have been verified by anyone who ever spent a week-end or a holiday in London. Being a weekend, all the businessmen would be away, their offices locked. Of the residents, those who were lucky enough to have country homes would undoubtedly be there. Moreover it was the Sunday of Christmas Week. Many normal weekend residents would have spent Christmas away, and would be making a long weekend of it, especially with the festivities of New Year's Eve to come. Of those that remained in London, few would feel inclined to do any fire-watching tonight. When the Luftwaffe dropped its clusters of fire bombs, there would be no one to put them out until the Fire Brigade arrived. By that time, it just might be too late.

After weighing all the factors, pro and con, the weather and the tides, but especially swayed by his own anger and craving for revenge, Adolf Hitler decided to give the order for London tonight. He would give them a New Year they would not forget for a long time to come. Hitler notified Göring of his decision, who notified General Hans Jeschonnek, the Luftwaffe Chief of Staff, who, in turn, rang up Generalfeldmarschall Hugo Sperrle in his suite at the Hotel Luxembourg in Paris. The wheels had been put in motion.

Hitler's information regarding the sparseness of the population of Central London on this Sunday was accurate. The number of people within the City district's boundaries was, by proportion, even more inadequate to meet the threat, a fact that would not have escaped the attention of the Nazi high command. There were only a few thousand residents, making the district one of the most underpopulated urban areas in Britain.

Most of the City's permanent inhabitants were 'house-keepers', full-time caretakers of the large, flat-roofed office blocks who lived on the premises. The presence of housekeepers was not just a wartime measure. Many families had lived in the same office building for years; the addition of roof-spotting duties had been a wartime expedient. Mr and Mrs Ing were permanent housekeepers of an office block at 34 Lime Street, near Lloyds Bank. Over near Finsbury Circus, the Bayliss family looked after a building at London Wall. Maybe it was because there were so few of them, or maybe it had something to do with the district, but residents of the City of London tended to be much more insular — with a village pride that sometimes bordered on fierceness — than the residents of any other London district.

The children of City families had a fine time playing in the deserted streets and back alleys on a Sunday like this. The narrow, criss-crossing lanes and dead-end courts, which exasperated 'foreigners' with their ins and outs, were a delight to moppets on skates. Dyers Court and Fountain Court, next to Guildhall, were favourites of scooter-powered children. The alleyways by the padlocked warehouses on Jewin Street and Redcross Street were as safe as playgrounds.

The City's streets had been widened and straightened over the centuries, as the district evolved from a walled mediaeval community to a business and banking capital, but their names did not change. The names of many of the district's thoroughfares hark back to the early Middle Ages. Cheapside takes its name from the Anglo-Saxon word *ceap*, or market — for centuries, Cheapside was London's market street. Avenues running into Cheapside were called after the goods that were sold there: Honey Lane was where beekeepers had their shops; Bread Street was lined with bakeshops; Panyar Alley, after the *panyars*, or basket-weavers, who lived there; Friday Street after the fishmongers, who sold their wares there on Friday. Whitecross Street was so-called because of a large white market cross, the local meeting place of the district, that stood at its northern end. Another such cross, this one red, stood north of Redcross Street. Jewin Street and Jewin Crescent mark the site of the Jewish burial ground during the twelfth and thirteenth centuries. The etymology of the Barbican, a roadway running eastward off Aldersgate, goes back even further. This street is named after a Roman watchtower *barbicana*, which stood in the vicinity in the first century.

The focal point of the City of London is St Paul's Cathedral, Sir Christopher Wren's masterpiece. Wren began construction of the Cathedral in 1675, replacing old St Paul's, which had been completely destroyed in the Great Fire of 1666. Thirty-five years later, in 1710, the building was completed. Its massive, lead-sheathed dome, now one of the most famous landmarks in the world, was criticised in the eighteenth century for being too unconventional, a defect which Londoners soon learned to overlook. Nearly as famous as its dome are the tombs and monuments within St Paul's. Among those buried in the Cathedral are the Duke of Wellington, who defeated Napoleon at the Battle of Waterloo, and Lord Horatio Nelson, the hero of Trafalgar, as well as Sir Christopher Wren, whose tomb occupies a central position. St Paul's had been damaged by bombs during October's nightly strings of air raids, but had suffered no serious structural damage.

Sunday morning services were still a weekly ritual for quite a few of the City's residents. There were certainly enough churches to choose from — forty-seven, to be exact — within the Square

Mile. Some had been badly damaged by bombs, notably St Mary-
le-Bow on Cheapside, famous for its Bow Bells, but most were
intact and active. There was elegant St Bride's, the printers'
church, in Fleet Street, and Christchurch, Greyfriars on Newgate Street. Picturesquely sombre St Giles Cripplegate, the burial
place of the poet John Milton and the Elizabethan explorer and
navigator Sir Martin Frobisher, lay just across the street from
Redcross Street Fire Station. St Mary the Virgin, Aldermanbury,
although plain and squat, boasted a lovely open courtyard and
garden, as well as the tombs of two actors named Heminge and
Condell, who were the first to gather and publish the plays of their
fellow actor, William Shakespeare, in 1623. There were no church
bells this morning, a casualty of the war. The ringing of church
bells throughout the land was the pre-arranged signal that the
feared German invasion had begun.

Church was a regular Sunday tradition for Olive Bayliss, the
young daughter of the London Wall housekeeper. Her church was
St Stephen's, Coleman Street, designed by Christopher Wren,
situated one block to the east of Guildhall. Although St Stephen's
was not as magnificent as many of Wren's churches, and was
sometimes dismissed as being plain and prosaic, it was well loved
by its loyal parishoners. As she rushed off to church, Miss Bayliss
could not have known that this morning's service would be the last
one ever held there.

Besides its picturesque halls and churches, the City also had its
share of military targets — all rated top priority by the Luftwaffe.
Prime targets for Nazi bombs were the three bridges across the
River Thames — Blackfriars, Southwark, and London Bridge, as
well as Tower Bridge, which is actually just outside the City
Boundary — and the railway bridge across Ludgate Hill, which
frequently carried trainloads of munitions. The six railway stations
within the City had also been marked by the Luftwaffe. The City's
concentration of telephone exchanges made the district uniquely
valuable to Britain's war effort. Of extreme importance to the
island's communications were the Wood Street Telephone Exchange and the London Telephone Service in the Faraday Building,
with its overseas trunk lines, as well as the General Post Office.
Each of these buildings, which were important enough to rate

pinpoint bombing attacks as separate targets, were within walking distance of each other other.

Most of these buildings had no full-time staff to look after them. In December of 1940, fire-spotting — the posting of a roof-top watch to extinguish fires and incendiary bombs — was purely voluntary; the majority of City firms, including railway stations and telephone exchanges, simply did not bother.

This was a dangerously irresponsible practice in view of the City's vulnerability — and military importance. The London Fire Brigade had labelled the district a 'fire zone' many years before. In peace-time, when firemen were able to concentrate on a single blaze, City fires were the most stubborn in London. Some City combustions, such as the great Barbican fire, were almost legendary among firemen. The chief fire hazard was the district's large number of gloomy, and highly combustible Victorian and Edwardian buildings. These old buildings, usually brick or stone on the outside but great heaps of timber — wooden staircases, roofing beams, floorboards, and the like — on the inside, were the bane of the Fire Brigade. One spark, it seemed, was enough to set these old dowagers alight.

The buildings in Paternoster Row, the area just to the north of St Paul's Cathedral, were typical. Most of these were flat, slate-roofed structures with wooden interiors, many of which dated from the end of the last century, that were packed with textiles, books, and other highly inflammable goods. Separated from one another by only a few yards in some cases, they were built so closely together that sunlight was smothered in the alleys between even on the brightest of days. Paternoster Square was the heart of the publishing and bookselling industry: over five million volumes were stored within its bounds.

If a fire started in one of these buildings, flames could jump across to another with amazing deftness. Once started, the fire would take hold and burn with stubborn intensity, defying the Fire Brigade's most determined efforts. One fireman called these old places 'torches looking for a light'.

The strict security observed by the owners in the bolting and locking of these office blocks and textile firms did not help the situation.

At least one firm in Paternoster Row had a fire crew on duty. A few yards north of the Cathedral, at 69/70 St Paul's Churchyard, Gordon Papps was having the same uneventful Sunday as always at his company, the textile firm Hitchcock, Williams & Co. Ltd. He lived on the premises, and spent most of his off-duty time in the firm's recreation room, which provided the staff members with entertainment during the dull hours. The radio was popular, although there wasn't much to listen to on Sunday morning. There were card games and innumerable cups of tea, and the gramophone was kept busy all day long. Papps was not given to music, but he could not ignore one particular tune, 'Deep in the Heart of Texas', which was played over and over. Another favourite of the time, Vera Lynn's vocal rendition of 'A Nightingale Sang in Berkeley Square', was as fanciful as its title — these days, Berkeley Square, in the West End near Piccadilly, was inhabited by a very un-romantic anti-aircraft gun.

Just' across the Courtyard from Hitchcock, Williams & Co., George Garwood, on duty at St Paul's Cathedral, had hardly any time to rest. A member of the St Paul's Cathedral Watch, Garwood ranged all over the Cathedral's roofs and the galleries of the great dome. From the Golden Gallery, the uppermost of the dome's two balconies, well over three hundred feet above the pavement, he had an unparalleled view in spite of this morning's overcast sky. On a clear day, he was able to see for miles in all directions.

The streets and lanes surrounding the Cathedral have histories as intriguing as the other avenues of the ancient district. Most took their names from pre-Reformation times, when the clergy of St Paul's walked round the outside chanting prayers on Corpus Christi day. The Creed was chanted in Creed Lane, the Hail Mary in Ave Maria Lane, the Lord's Prayer in Paternoster Row, and the procession came to its end in Amen Court. Paternoster Row had been the hub of the publishing industry for many centuries, certainly before 1666; the booksellers suffered heavy losses of property in the Great Fire.

For every firm like Hitchcock, Williams & Co., and every building like St Paul's Cathedral, that voluntarily posted roof spotters, there were scores that did not. Station Officer Laurence J. Odling of Whitefriars Fire Station covered the issue squarely, saying that fire watchers were 'very much in the missing'. Most places had no one at all to look after things at night or on weekends, not even a custodian. The Sandra Hat Company, a small firm on Whitecross Street, was typical. When the factory finished work, the owner-manager closed it up and left for home. The building had no night staff, and so was completely deserted.

It was no coincidence that five fire stations lay within the City's boundaries. The stations were situated so that fire appliances — the fireman's term for fire engines — would be able to reach an an outbreak of fire within a few minutes. Along with the fire-houses there was also a Salvage Corps Station on Watling Street, the oldest thoroughfare in the district, and an Ambulance Station near Smithfield Close, where Protestant martyrs were burnt alive in the sixteenth century by the devoutly Catholic Queen Mary Tudor. The number of fire and civil defence stations within the district were ample testimony to the City's unprotected state.

Every fireman in each of the City's fire stations knew the district street by street, alley by alley — no mean feat considering the Square Mile's Chinese puzzle of avenues. The location of every hydrant also was memorised; in the dark of night, there was no time to search for water. In peace-time it was bad enough. Now, with the blackout and the Nazi bombs to contend with, a difficult job became even worse.

Inside the firehouses stood the fire engines, clean and ever so shiny. The fire pumps ranged in size from the Heavy Unit, capable of pumping close to 1,000 gallons per minute, to the turntable ladder, another large pump with a 100-foot extension ladder, down to the small but indispensable Coventry Climax and Dennis trailer pumps. These trailer pumps were just what their names implied — pumps on wheels. They did not even have engines to propel them, but had to be towed, usually by a taxi but occasion-ally by another large car. The almost exclusive use of trailer pumps by the Auxiliary Fire Service earned the post-1939 volunteers the dubious title, 'The Taxi Brigade'. Most fire appliances had their brilliant red finish covered by a lacklustre wartime grey, but this did not excuse firemen from keeping their machines polished to a glossy sheen. This was one chore a fireman could always look for-ward to — keeping his fire engine shiny and bright.

Fireman James Goldsmith of Redcross Street Fire Station

Sunday was no different from any other day for most firemen. In every station — Bishopsgate, Whitefriars, based at King's College on the Strand since the war broke out, Cannon Street, Embankment, in back of St Bride's Church, Redcross Street — it was always the same old routine. Fireman James Goldsmith, at Redcross Street Fire Station, was kept busy with his usual labours. There was always cleaning to be done around the station, and his fire appliance had to be kept polished. Also, the hydrants in the area had to be checked to make sure that everything was in working order, and his pump and equipment were always ready . . . just in case. These days, nobody knew what to expect, or when to expect it.

The planning session in Feldmarschall Hugo Sperrle's suite at the Hotel Luxembourg in Paris did not last much longer than most conferences. The bombing attack against London which the Feldmarschall and his staff had drawn up during the conference was to be much heavier than usual, however. As outlined, tonight's attack would be split into two waves. The first wave would consist of between 135 and 140 aircraft, which would drop a bomb load composed mostly of incendiaries, reducing the target area to a bubbling cauldron of flame. The second wave, slightly larger than the first, would attack with hundreds of 550 lb high-explosive bombs, stirring up the fires started by the first wave and, at the same time, making things very difficult for the firemen down below. Close to 300 sorties would be flown over London, quite a few of these being double sorties — each aircraft flying two trips — making it the heaviest attack on the British capital in well over a month.

Actually, Feldmarschall Sperrle was not all that keen on tonight's attack. Because of the solid blanket of cloud over London, his aircrews would not be able to see their target. The young pilots and navigators might fly well beyond their target and drop their bombs well off the mark, as had happened often enough in the past.

On a clear, moonlit night, London was lit up almost as brightly as during daylight. From the air, the face of Central London looked just as it did on the Luftwaffe's briefing maps. Landmarks could easily be picked out — the great dark patches that were Hyde Park and St James's Park, the Houses of Parliament, the Elephant and Castle's spider web of converging streets, the Millwall Docks near the 'U' bend in the River Thames, all stood out boldly in the revealing white light. On a night like tonight, however, when all of southern England would be hidden under heavy layers of clouds, the conscript pilots and bomb-aimers would not be able to see anything. It was entirely possible, Sperrle knew, that they might overfly their destinations completely, or at least enough of them to make a shambles of the bombing mission.

And tonight's target was no routine assignment. Feldmarschall Sperrle was directing his Air Fleet against the City of London, the ancient district with its concentration of railway stations, communications centres, and highly combustible buildings. This area had been high on the Luftwaffe's list for some time. Following last Sunday's particularly successful fire raid against Manchester, the time was ripe to use the same tactics against the City of London.

According to the operational blueprint, the first wave's fire bombs would create an inferno that would be visible for miles. This would give the second wave a target that would be almost impossible to miss, even for dead tired air crews on their second sortie of the night. Because of the conditions within the City, added to the low tides, this should not be very difficult to achieve.

The only problem was with the young and very green pilots and crews themselves, who made up a large portion of Luftflotte 3's staff. On a cloudless night with a full moon, St Paul's Cathedral provided a beacon that pointed out the City even from 15,000 feet up — the shape of its great Latin cross was practically impossible to overlook. But on this night, St Paul's would be invisible. The latest records from the meteorologists, now under the cold, steady stare of Feldmarschall Sperrle, offered no hope. The reports informed him that the weather was expected to remain the same way for at least twenty-four hours.

# CHAPTER TWO

# A Bit Blank
## *Afternoon*

Feldmarschall Sperrle could be certain that one of his units would reach and bomb the target, at least. For tonight's attack would be led by none other than *Kampf Gruppe* (Bomb Wing) 100, the 'glamour boy' outfit of the Luftwaffe's bomber fleet. This celebrated unit was justly famous throughout the German Air Force for having the best pilots and air crews, and was equally renowned for its exploits among the pundits of British Intelligence.

KG 100's fame was no accident. Nicknamed 'The Fire Raisers', KG 100 was a tough and battle-hardened Pathfinder wing. Its job was to drop thousands of fire bombs on the assigned target at the very beginning of an air raid, creating a brilliant 'bull's eye' for the rest of the Air Fleet to aim at. The men who belonged to this bomber wing were as unique as the job they performed. No 'hostilities only' gunners and navigators or untried boy pilots flew with this outfit. *Kampf Gruppe* 100 was staffed entirely by hand-picked officers, most of whom were pre-war Luftwaffe men and all having many hours of combat experience, constituting the élite of the Luftwaffe's bomber pilots and crews.

This singularly distinctive and colourful unit was based at Vannes, on the southern side of Brittany's gloomy, grey peninsula. Its leader was Hauptmann Friedrich Aschenbrenner, much decorated for bravery and a veteran of many bombing missions since the outbreak of the war. Aschenbrenner and his men operated a wing of twenty bombers, twin-engined Heinkel He111s, the Luftwaffe's standard, tried-and-true medium bomber. The He111 carried a crew of five and a bomb load of 4,400 lbs, with racks in its bomb bay for either eight 550 lb high-explosive bombs or eight canisters of incendiaries. Because of its lack of speed and range, the He111 was being replaced by the Junkers Ju88A, a faster and longer-legged bomber, which was also capable of carrying a heavier bomb load.

The bombers under Aschenbrenner's command were not the standard model, however, but were as special as everything else about his unit. KG100 flew He111 H2s, which were the same as the standard model except for one item: these aircraft were equipped with an electronic device that allowed its crew to find its target even on the darkest or foggiest of nights — the so-called 'X-apparatus'.

The X-apparatus was, simply stated, an invaluable, almost foolproof, electronic aid to navigation and precision bombing. The way in which it worked was far from simple, however. The radio receiver inside the aircraft picked up a high-frequency radio-direction beam which was transmitted from a station along the coast of Normandy. This beam, the 'primary beam' — sent from Station Anton, on the Cherbourg peninsula — was aimed by the Luftwaffe's Signal Corps so that it would pass directly over the appointed target. The bombers of KG 100 would simply fly along this 'primary' beam all the way to their target, just as a car is driven along a straight, well-paved roadway.

The radio operator was the key man while the aircraft was 'flying the beam'; only he could tell when the plane was beginning to stray off course. From his compartment behind the pilot, the radioman, his earphones plugged into the X-apparatus, listened intently. As long as he heard a low, constant buzz in his head-set, the aircraft was on course. If he heard a string of either dots or dashes, indicating that the bomber was straying to the left or right of their course, the radioman would notify the pilot that the aircraft was veering from the beam's pathway, and an adjustment would be made.

Along its course, the 'primary' beam was intersected by two other beams which were laid across it, crossing the 'X'. The first intersecting beam, broadcast from Station Cicero near Fécamp, Normandy, ninety miles up the coast from Station Anton, was the 'advance signal'. When the aircraft crossed this beam, it was an indication that the bomber was about ten miles from the target. The second cross beam, from Station Berta outside Calais, one hundred miles east of Station Cicero, was the 'main signal'. This beam announced that the aircraft was directly over the target area, and that the bomb aimer should drop his cargo. Free of its bomb

A flight of Heinkel He111s, 'the Luftwaffe's standard, tried-and-true medium bomber', on their way to England during one of the September raids.

A Junkers Ju 88 with external bomb racks under the wings. Called the 'wonder bomber' before the war, the Ju 88 was the best bomber in service with the Luftwaffe during the Blitz.

load, which made the He111 forty miles per hour faster, the aircraft would then be turned around and pointed towards its home base at Vannes.

Another system that made use of the X-apparatus was also employed, a much more sophisticated procedure by which the intersecting beams released the bomb load automatically. With this method, the pilot and radioman had to work even more closely together to put their bombs on the mark.

As soon as the aircraft passed through the first cross beam, the 'advance signal', a buzzing sound registered in the radio operator's earphones; he would then press a lever on a clock, starting a timer and engaging the automatic mechanism. While this timer was running, the pilot was obliged to keep a sharp eye on his ground speed — a precise rate of miles per hour had to be maintained if the automatic sequence was to work properly.

When this first clock ran out, the radioman engaged a second device, which was linked electronically to the bomb-release mechanism itself. After this had been done, the pilot was forced to follow an even more rigid flight pattern, which could not vary in either height or speed — anything but a comfortable time for everyone on board, since the aircraft was now a fish in a barrel for both night fighters and anti-aircraft fire. As the Heinkel passed through the 'main signal', this second cross beam activated the bomb-release device, toggling the bomb load electrically.

The X-apparatus virtually eliminated the possibility of human error among the bomber crews in precision bombing. British Intelligence would eventually find a way of tampering with the crossed radio beams, throwing the bombers off course, but this would not happen for several months. For now, the X-beams penetrated to the heart of England, clear, unobstructed highways for the Luftwaffe. As long as the beams themselves were laid carefully and accurately, the X-apparatus was virtually infallible.

Although the X-apparatus was too complex to be of any practical use by most bomber crews, especially during the excitement and strain of battle, it worked to perfection when used by an expert and highly-trained crew — such as the veterans of KG100. The first time that Hauptmann Aschenbrenner and his *Gruppe* tested the X-apparatus on an actual bombing mission had been only six weeks before, on the night of 14th November. The target on that night had been Coventry — the fires set by KG100 had rung up the curtain on one of the most destructive terror attacks of the Blitz against Britain.

On this Sunday, Hauptmann Aschenbrenner would have received his wing's operational orders by early afternoon, before one o'clock. The official communiqué announced that this night's bombing objective would be London, and, as usual, he and his group would spearhead the attack, going in low and fast to light up the assigned area with incendiary bombs. The Target Area within Loge (the code-name for London) was the City of London, with its hodgepodge of old buildings — tailor-made for Aschenbrenner's 'Fire Raisers'.

Aschenbrenner had the same misgivings about the weather as Feldmarschall Hugo Sperrle, only more practical — Sperrle's worries were purely objective, while Aschenbrenner would actually have to fly through it. Even though he was a veteran of many bombing sorties, Aschenbrenner did not look forward to bombing through a layer of clouds. It was always bad enough on a clear night. The X-apparatus would certainly be a help tonight. On most sorties, the radio beams that guided him right to the target, and even triggered his bombs, were nothing more than an elaborate luxury. On this night, when he would not be able to see his target, they would be a necessity.

The operational orders for Kampf Gruppe 100 went on to decide a host of other details: bomb load; take-off time; altitude. The bomb load was standard: eight canisters of incendiaries for each of the He111s. Each canister held 36 of the foot-long fire-bombs, making a total of 288 bombs per aircraft — the entire wing, twenty aircraft in all, would drop close to 6,000 of them. Take-off time would be at 5.30 p.m.; according to Hauptmann Aschenbrenner's calculations, he should reach his target by about 7.05 p.m. (British time was one hour earlier than the Continent. Aschenbrenner would be arriving at about 6.05, London time.) Cruising altitude would be 6,000 feet, which came as no great surprise. KG100 always went in at low level.

Looking over the operations map for the hundredth time, Aschenbrenner took a few more notes. His He111 H2 would cross the English coastline at a point about five miles east of the town of Bognor Regis, in West Sussex. The approach to the target would be from the south-west. As the commander of the élite bombing wing, Aschenbrenner would have the job of filling in the other seventy-nine pilots and crewmen of the *Gruppe* with the details of tonight's attack — nobody else except the staff officers even knew that a mission was slated — but it was still early. There would be plenty of time before he would have to order them to assemble in the briefing room. He could, at least, allow everyone to finish their lunch.

Mr A.W.F. Grafton and his fiancée Dorothy Hyland, both of East Ham in East London, were planning to attend a friend's birthday party. Both of them liked to dance, and enjoyed singing around the old piano, which had several notes missing but still managed to sound tuneful. The celebration promised to be a pleasantly noisy and lively time, and they both looked forward to the festivities.

The afternoon sky was grey and bleak, making the day as gloomy as it was cold. But the weather did not bother Mr Grafton. In fact, the glaze of overcast reassured him. The solid layer of cloud cover was a sign that there might not be an 'early siren' tonight; since he and Dorothy would be walking to the birthday party, an air raid alert would put an abrupt end to their planned evening.

This party was probably the liveliest thing on in London tonight. It was not just because it was a Sunday; there wasn't much doing on any other night, either. The bombings had severely curbed evening activities, but there were a good many people who would have run the risk of being caught in an air raid to find some entertainment. The petrol shortage also inhibited night travel. But there was one conspicuous reason why Londoners stayed indoors after dark: the black-out.

Everybody condemned the black-out; when people were in a good mood, they called it a 'damn nuisance'. A woman from Middlesex was somewhat more bitter about the restrictions imposed upon her daily activities, complaining that the completely unlit streets only allowed her to live 'half a life'. But after six-teen months of war, most people had grown used to it, or at least resigned themselves to it. American reporters sometimes made a game of the whole thing, playing a kind of blind man's bluff in the darkness. As they rode through the claustrophobic darkness in taxis (when they could find one), they took turns in attempting to pick out buildings and landmarks. They were usually not very successful.

Most Londoners found the imposed black-out far less entertaining. Street kerbs and the bases of lamp posts were painted white, but this did not prevent some unlucky souls from tripping off the pavement in the darkness and turning an ankle. Air Raid Wardens, keeping an irritatingly sharp eye out for the slightest chink of light that might peer from behind window blinds or blackout curtains, likewise did not help to soothe a person's temper or sweeten his disposition. The ARP men had no qualms at all over rousing an offender from a warm armchair, pounding on the door and bellowing 'You've got a light showing!'

The dusk to dawn blackness was a fact of life, however, and people learned to live with it. Some forced themselves to find certain aspects of the black-out romantic, even enjoyable. The complete absence of street lamps and illuminated signs made the sky seem deeper and mysteriously beautiful. Mrs Ernest Boyd of Sydenham recalls that she 'never saw so many stars'.

On this Sunday, 29th December, the black-out went into effect at 5.26 p.m. and lasted until 8.38 a.m. — a total of fifteen hours and twelve minutes. Underneath the weary resignation shown by most Londoners lurked a growing feeling of unhappiness and depression because of the imposed darkness. The 14th December edition of *Picture Post* featured a two-page spread of photos of New York City, 'Where the Christmas Lights Still Shine', graphically displaying the gaudy lights of Broadway and the brightly illuminated George Washington Bridge. The caption that accompanies the pictures ominously narrates, 'Over in New York the lights still shine — for how long no one can say.'

BBC commentator Robin Duff, writing in the periodical *London Calling*, had an equally inauspicious point of view.

I am almost dreading the day when the lights of London are switched on again. As we grope our way through the black-

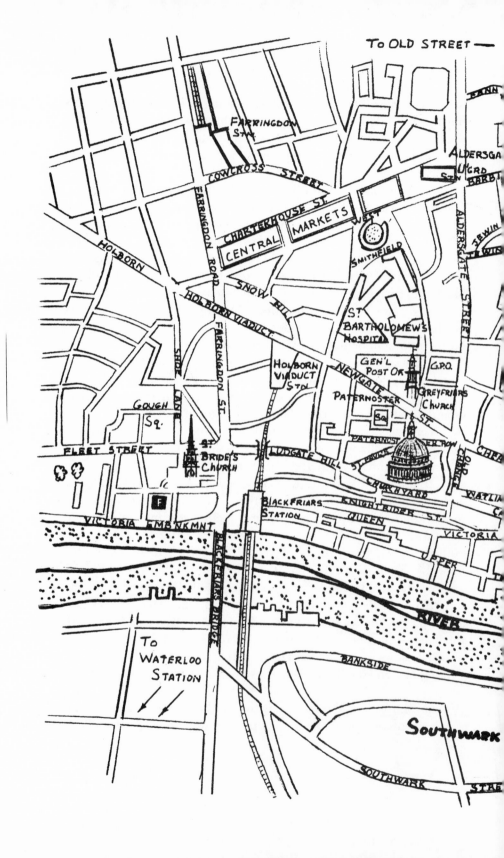

out, we can at least cling to our memories of what London was. When that curtain is lifted . . . we shall find that the London we remembered is only a shadow.

People had already found that the West End wasn't what it used to be, especially on Sunday. Films were immensely popular, although people usually went in the afternoon so that they could be home before black-out. There were plenty of films to be seen around town. Charles Chaplin was packing in the crowds with *The Great Dictator* at both the Gaumont Cinema, in the Haymarket, and at the Marble Arch Pavilion. The glorified pantomime *The Thief of Baghdad*, with Conrad Veidt, was at the Odeon Cinema, Leicester Square. Just across the square at the Empire, Judy Garland and Mickey Rooney cavorted in *Strike Up The Band*. Bette Davis and Charles Boyer starred in *All This And Heaven Too* at the Warner Cinema.

A few live theatres were occupied, although pickings among shows was slim indeed. The almost total lack of decent plays moved one critic to proclaim, in a beautifully low-key statement, that London theatre 'lacked excitement', and went on to add that life in general was 'a bit blank' this Christmas season. Actually, Christmas week saw twelve shows in the West End, more than there had been in months. This morning's edition of *The Observer* noted that the shows have been 'well attended', and that box office queues have been seen at some of them.

Most of the shows were either variety-reviews or escapist-theme plays. All of them had daytime performances. Mrs Frances Hine of Isleworth, Middlesex, had booked seats for herself and her two children at tomorrow afternoon's performance of *Where the Rainbow Ends*, at the New Theatre. Prices: 1 shilling to 6 shillings and sixpence.* The *Second Programme of 'Diversion'* was on stage at Wyndham's Theatre. The title 'diversion' was taken from an increasingly evident London street sign re-directing traffic away from bomb craters.

At the Windmill, the young lovelies were on stage 'Continuous daily from 11.15 a.m. to 7.30 p.m.' The show was called *Revudeville*, now in its fifth week. The Windmill's line of leggy chorus

*5 to 32½ New Pence; 20¢ to $1.30 in US currency.

girls strutted and kicked right through the Blitz, prompting the management to adopt the slogan, 'We're Never Closed'. Since the Windmill was best known for its bevy of nudes, the local wits soon changed the slogan to, 'We're Never Clothed'.

The nude review might have been a morale booster for the audience, but working after black-out at the height of the Blitz was no balm to the girls' nerves. When one of the young ladies was asked how she felt when appearing nude on stage, she replied that she felt more naked than ever when a bomb landed close by. She wondered what lucky officer or man would get a couple of legs in case of a direct hit. If the girls did not enjoy the working conditions, some members of the audience weren't wild about the show, either. One man, a chaplain, was heard to say that he thought someone must be forcing them on stage with a gun.

On Sunday, the West End was almost totally lacking in forms of amusement. Most people went to church in the morning, or else slept late, and spent the afternoon reading the newspapers. On 29th December the headlines did their best to sound encouraging, although there was not very much to be enthusiastic about. The heading on page seven of *The Observer* proclaimed, '100 Bombs a Minute Raid: Invasion Ports Plastered.' The column went on to report that 'wave after wave' of R A F bombers had pounded French ports and long-range gun positions across the Channel in night-long attacks. Because the weather had lately been foggy and overcast, these strikes were the heaviest in over a week.

This news came as not only a source of grim satisfaction for Londoners, who had endured over 450 air raids since September, but also graphic evidence that Hitler's threat to invade Britain was still taken very seriously. The editorial columns of yesterday's, Saturday, 28th December's, edition of the *News Chronicle* asked, 'Will Invasion Come?' The editors decided that it was more than possible.

Reports from abroad were much brighter. British troops were gaining ground on all fronts in the North African desert. During the past week, the army had surrounded two Italian garrisons on the Mediterranean coast of Libya, and had taken hordes of prisoners. The headline on page seven cast a hopeful look toward the other side of the Atlantic: 'ROOSEVELT'S PLAN TO AID

BRITAIN: Plain Words In Tonight's 'Fireside Talk' '. The report went on to say that US President Franklin D. Roosevelt was expected to outline his policy of aid to Britain tonight at 9.00, Washington, DC time, in his latest 'Fireside Chat'. Roosevelt's speech was expected to be of 'extreme importance', according to the staff of *The Observer*, clarifying America's plan contribution to Britain's war effort.

The papers were filled with advertisements for the coming January sales, many of which were slated to begin tomorrow, 30th January. The wartime shortage of goods made this season's sales somewhat controversial. Most shops argued that the sales were good for business, and that women looked forward to them all year. But some stores wanted to cut them out altogether, protesting that sales would make the coming high prices seem even worse.

Controversy or not, Selfridges was beginning its sale on Monday, 'for six days only'. Model coats would be selling for £5 and £6, and day gowns for £2, £3, or £4 pounds each. John Barker & Co. Ltd., High Street, Kensington, was pricing its men's worsted suits at five pounds. Marshall & Snellgrove, exclusive ladies' shop on Oxford Street, announced that its sale would begin next Monday, 6th January, 'Despite abnormal conditions and rising prices'.

A few weeks earlier, Simpsons, the famous steak house on the Strand noted for its robust and straightforward cuisine, did not serve sirloin of beef for the first time since the restaurant opened. This was such a noteworthy event that it made the daily newspapers. The reason for this shortcoming was simple: no beef was available.

It seemed that every passing week brought a shortage of something else: onions, tea, sugar, and especially 'non-essential' items like glassware and linens. The shortage of silk for stockings and lingerie earlier in December, caused by the silk industry's switch to war production, made a bad situation even worse. Every lingerie shop and counter in London was mobbed by hordes of scrambling, shoving women after the cutback had been announced. To the average shopper at Harrods and Derry & Toms, the shortages were almost as bad as the German bombers.

*

At Luftwaffe airfields all across northern France, teletype machines clacked out the news of tonight's mission. In Brittany, II Wing of *Kampfgeschwader* (Bomb Group) 27, based at Dinard, and III Wing of KG27, further inland at Rennes — I Wing of KG54 at Evreux and II Wing of the same *Geschwader* at St André in Normandy — three wings of *Lehrgeschwader* (Demonstration Bomb Group) 1 at Orléans — II Wing of KG51 at Orly, outside Paris — all got the word: 'London again tonight'.

As word of the air strike was announced, the pilots and air-crews of the various bomber groups turned to look up at the grey sky, studying the heavy overcast sky. None of these units was equipped with the X-apparatus, and would have to find their own way to the target without any electronic aids and bomb visually, so their reaction to flying a bombing mission in bad weather was predictable. Some of the men shook their heads in disbelief — how could anyone order them to fly in this weather? Some, more outspoken, complained out loud, not only about the weather but also about their superior officers' mental competency. Others resigned themselves to their fate in silence, not daring to question an order. Still others secretly hoped that the clouds would continue to thicken and that a hard, steady downpour would inundate the airfield, forcing a cancellation of the mission.

The youthful and largely untried navigators, gunners, and pilots were the most apprehensive. KG100's veterans might toss off this evening's planned sortie as just another mission, but the young 'hostilities only' gunners and bomb-aimers of Air Fleet Three were far from being veterans. These youngsters were usually a keen lot, although keenness was hardly a substitute for experience on a night bombing run. Today, even their eagerness was missing. Many were only weeks, or even days, out of training school; as the Luftwaffe replaced its losses and expanded to cover planned operations in the Balkans and North Africa, the *Luftflotte* were forced to rely heavily upon 'hostilities only' personnel and fast, concentrated courses of training. Only a year before, many of the pimply-faced kids who now wore the eagle insignia of the Luft-waffe were only just out of school or still living on the farm. Flying a combat mission in bad weather brought a plague of doubts to mind: 'How are we supposed to know when we've

crossed the English coast?' they thought. 'How are we supposed
to see the target?' Worse still, 'What if the weather worsens while
we're away — how are we supposed to land on runways we can't
even find?'

As was always the case, it was the seasoned pilots, the pre-
war Luftwaffe navigators, the bomb-aimers who had flown combat
missions over France and Poland and the Low Countries, who
held the line. These veteran officers — Major Winkler of II Wing,
KG51 at Orly; Hauptmann Wilhelm Kern of Number 1 Wing,
LG1 at Orleans — came into their own when the situation was
tight and anxious, knowing the answers to the many and complex problems of combat flying as only experience can teach
them, instilling confidence in the young fledgelings. Sometimes,
this involved nothing more, and nothing less, than talking them
out of their fears.

The nineteen- and twenty year-old navigators were exhorted
to rely upon their recently-learned training — a few clouds were
not going to change the points on the compass! The cloud cover
worked both ways, the green bomb-aimers were told; if they could
not see the ground, then the enemy anti-aircraft gunners would
not be able to see them, either. The kids were often jokingly reassured that they were better off in the Luftwaffe, where they had
warm beds and hot food and beer in the officers' mess, than they
would be in the navy, seasick on the stormy Atlantic, or in the
army, where it was mud and drill and hard rations all the time.
After a few minutes of talk with their superiors on the realities
of operational flying, all of the youngsters' fears might not have
vanished entirely, but at least they were reduced to their proper
proportions.

Any doubts and misgivings were lost in the scramble of preparing
for the mission. First on the list was the pre-strike briefing, which
was no great comfort to anyone on this afternoon. Pilots and
crews, sitting row upon row in the long briefing rooms, were
casually informed that there would be overcast sky over London,
as well as all the way over there and all the way back. There was,
however, one resounding note of encouragement — the 'Fire
Raisers' of KG100 would be going in first, setting fires that would
be visible for miles despite the overcast. The pathfinders of KG100

were well-known throughout the Luftwaffe for their expertise, not without a fair share of jealous envy. If the 'glamour boys' could light up the target the way they did at Coventry, then, at least, there should be no problem in hitting the assigned area.

The briefing ritual varied from group to group, from almost pompous ceremony to easygoing informality, but the same salient points were touched upon at every airfield. The target was described: the City of London – telephone exchanges and warehouses and railway yards – important to Britain's war effort. The fact that the bomb load would consist largely of incendiaries came as something of a surprise, even after last Sunday's Manchester raid. The target, it was explained, was made up of mostly old buildings that would burn easily. Their job was to set it alight, to re-create the Great Fire of London, providing an aiming point for further attacks later in the night. This last point struck a harsh chord. It sounded as though two sorties might be ordered for tonight. Nobody liked to make two trips.

Every wing was assigned its own altitude level, ranging between 10,000 and 16,000 feet, in order to lessen the danger of a mid-air collision. Above 12,000 feet, anti-aircraft fire was not much of a problem – the flak rarely hit anything, anyway, but could throw a young bomb-aimer off his mark if the shooting was heavy enough – but night-fighters could be a bother. Not that night fighters were any great menace, either. Despite the fact that they were equipped with radar sets, the fighters hardly ever found the intruding bombers. When a fighter pilot did manage to spot an enemy bomber, he had to creep up stealthily on his prey. For even though the British night fighters had air-to-air radar, and were in touch with ground-based radar stations as well, a bomber that spotted an approaching fighter and took violent evasive action was almost certain to break away from its pursuer. The real danger lay in crashing into another bomber, hence the strictness about altitudes.

While the briefing was going on, the bombs and bullets that would be used in tonight's attack were wheeled out of the magazines and loaded aboard the waiting aircraft. There was an occasional 550 lb high-explosive bomb, dark and squat with jutting tail fins, mixed in with the long, cylindrical 'molotov Breadbaskets', but incendiaries were the order of the day. The exact bomb load depended upon each individual group, or more exactly, whether the bomb group flew the Heinkel He111 or the more modern Junkers Ju88. Kampfgeschwader 51 and 54 were equipped with the newer Ju88As, while KG55 and KG27 still flew the old reliable He111. The Ju88 held a maximum twelve canisters of incendiaries in its bomb load, compared with the eight in the He111, and could carry over two thousand pounds more of high-explosive bombs than the Heinkel. Although the Junkers had a much more feeble defensive armament — the Ju88A had only one 7.90 mm. machine gun, compared with three swivel mounted guns in the He111 — it was faster by far than any other bomber in the Luftwaffe. Its 'on paper' maximum speed was 416 mph, and had an extended cruising radius.

Originally, the Luftwaffe general staff had planned to replace every He111 in all the bomb groups with the Junkers aircraft, but the transformation was taking longer than the high command expected. When the twin-engine Junkers Ju88 first appeared in 1937, it was labelled the 'wonder bomber' — not only could it fly faster and longer and carry more bombs than the He111, but also, the experts said, it was so fast that it could outrun any enemy fighter. (This accounts for the single machine gun.) This last item was spoken a trifle prematurely. The Spitfires and Hurricanes managed to catch up with the Ju88 and, 'wonder bomber' or not, it proved no less vulnerable to the streams of .303 tracer ammunition from the British fighters than the somewhat moss-grown Heinkel bomber.

As the bomb-handlers and armourers went about their jobs, routinely and systematically, the tension and anxiety inside each of the large, sterile briefing rooms grew more stifling with every passing minute. Row upon row of men, some sporting small, well-trimmed moustaches, but mostly clean-shaven with closely cropped hair, gazed intently at the uniformed figure standing on the small stage in front of them, hanging on his every word. The tension inside each of them was not the dread caused by self-doubt, for even the fledgeling pilots and gunners were beyond that point by now, but was the realisation that in a few hours they would be doing their best to set fire to the largest and most populous city in England, and that the British would be doing their equal best to stop them.

Even the old hands, the veterans of many missions, listened more closely as the Wing Commander described the target, and the meteorologist jabbed at the huge wall map with his pointer. All of the Wing Commander's comments and the weatherman's scientific jargon boiled down to one cold, hard fact: this would be no easy bombing mission. The ten-tenths cloud density that covered most of northern Europe was far more than just uncomfortable for flying; it was dangerous. After the meteorologist finished, tonight's codes were announced — identification codes, radio codes, call signals, light signals — and jotted down.

The briefing finally ended; everyone snapped to attention as the Wing Commander and his executive officer strode down the aisle, and the assembly was dismissed. But the pilots and aircrew members still had two rituals to perform. First, there was queueing up for parachutes. Next, everyone received their 'flight rations', mostly high-energy foods, such as chocolate, nuts, and dried fruit, that could be stuffed into jacket pockets, as well as a few pep pills and caffeine tablets.

After all of that was done and out of the way, there was nothing more to do until take-off time except wait. How long a man had to wait depended upon which bomber group he belonged to. KG100 was scheduled to go at 5.30; [4.30 London time]* Hauptmann Aschenbrenner and his crack pilots had only a short while to bide. The last units would not leave until 10.45, [9.45 London time] and still had several hours. No one had been told yet that this was a double strike mission. The High Command reasoned, correctly, that the men would only worry excessively if they knew that two trips to the target were scheduled, and their worrying would adversely affect their performance. Those slated to fly two sorties would be told when the time came.

The young Leutnants and Oberleutnants and non-commissioned officers filtered back to their huts. Inside, they sat and talked about places they had been before the war, or girls they had known; smoked cigarettes; played cards; slept. Anything to keep their minds off tonight.

*Luftwaffe take-off time was one hour later than London time.

No one in London had any inkling of what lay in store for them. The Luftwaffe's recent visits gave no sign that Adolf Hitler and the Luftwaffe High Command had any special plans on for tonight; the last heavy raid had been on 8th December, nearly three weeks ago. Friday night's bombing had been typical of recent raids — short and scattered. The bomber force had dropped a mix of high-explosive and incendiary bombs over a wide area of the metropolis in an attack that lasted about two hours. As usual, the anti-aircraft batteries blasted away at the attackers all through the raid, but, as usual, the only damage they inflicted was upon the eardrums of the local residents.

But the rest of this past week had been quiet, save for Sunday's light attack. Both Christmas Eve and Christmas Day, as well as Boxing Day, had been raid free. When the Luftwaffe did not come over on Christmas, most people were amazed; a holiday attack was just the sort of thing they had come to expect. Air-raid shelters were quiet and subdued, as though the residents were straining to hear the strident warning of the sirens. In the deep shelters of the Underground stations, the mood was livened up a bit by the Salvation Army Carol Choir, which toured the stations with their traditional Christmas songs.

Some brave individuals didn't care if the bombers came or not; they refused to spend Christmas in an air raid shelter. Prompted by the recent lull in enemy activity, they declared that they would 'risk one night at home', come what may. The most conspicuous reaction to the Luftwaffe's failure to appear was surprise rather than relief. A woman in Ilford, Essex made these entries in her pocket diary:

December 24th — Tuesday: 'No raids (wonder of wonders)'
December 25th — Wednesday, Xmas: 'They gave us a peaceful day with *NO RAIDS*'

Since 7th September, when the East End docks were bombed and heavily damaged, London had spent over 1,200 hours under fire. People went on with their daily lives as best they could, and British industry publicly dismissed their bomb damage as unimportant, but after nearly four months the regular bombing raids were beginning to tell.

Newspaper accounts often gave the impression that only hospitals, churches, and other non-military targets were hit, mainly because of strictly enforced censorship that prevented reporters from writing detailed accounts of bomb damage. Besides the docks, however, scattered power plants, gas works, railway stations, telephone exchanges, and a good many factories had also suffered heavily. On 7th November, Parliament was forced to assemble in a new, 'unspecified' place. After the chambers had been hit twice by bombs, it was decided that the Palace of Westminster offered too good a target.

The Members of Parliament were not the only ones who left. A good many Londoners, mostly those from the wealthier classes, who could afford to go, fled to the country. Houses all over Greater London were empty; in Chelsea, entire rows of homes stood vacant. For those who stayed, safety from air attacks became the prominent thought concerning nightly lodgings. The sturdiness of a hotel's air raid shelter now ranked in importance with the comfort of its rooms and the efficiency of its staff. These advertisements appeared in this morning's *Observer*:

*London's Fireproof Hotel*, the Eccleston, Eccleston Sq. S.W.1. *Reinforced Concrete Building*. Splendid shelters and heated underground. Rooms from 7 shillings.*

*St Ermin's, Westminster*. An address of distinction. Renowned for quietude and comfort. Fully Licensed Restaurant. Comfortable Lounge. Central Heating. Strongly reinforced Air Raid Shelter. Special Terms arranged for H.M. Forces. Bedroom and Breakfast from 10s 6d.**

The main topic around town today was the respite from the bombing, and how soon the attacks would start again. After nearly four months of the Blitz the lull was a source of uneasiness. The bombs were expected, but peace and quiet made everyone suspicious. Special Constable R.E. Crowfoot, walking his beat in the City, recalled that the enemy 'did much of his work' on week-

*35 New Pence; $1.40 US Dollars.

**52½ New Pence, $2.10 US Dollars.

ends. When the docks were heavily bombed in the first of London's air raids, Constable Crowfoot had also been on duty. 7th and 8th September had been a Saturday and Sunday.

The twenty He111s of Kampf Gruppe 100 slumped heavily upon their three landing wheels at the airfield of Vannes, Brittany, fuelled-up and armed. In each of the aircraft, eight 'Molotov Breadbaskets' nestled snugly in their racks. The dorsal 7.90 machine gun and the ventral gun, pointing aft from behind the bomb bay, were loaded and ready. Each of the four fuel tanks, holding 760 Imperial Gallons between them, had been topped off. The mechanics and armourers and the other members of the ground crew had done their jobs, and the fate of the evening's venture was now out of their hands.

Shortly before 5 p.m. [4 p.m. London time] the air crews began arriving at their flight stations. Hauptmann Friedrich Aschenbrenner reached his aircraft, settled into the pilot's seat and unceremoniously began ticking off the items on the cockpit check list, one at a time: bomb-bay doors; flaps; intercom; switches; gauges. When he was satisfied that everything checked out properly, Aschenbrenner started each of the Heinkel's 1,100 horsepower engines. The port engine slowly came to life with a burst of blue exhaust smoke and a prolonged, high-pitched cough that quickly changed to a growl and then a roar as the three-blade airscrew whirled at an increasing tempo. The same chain of events was repeated when the starboard engine was engaged, while Aschenbrenner listened carefully for any sign of hesitation in the loud, steady din that bathed the cockpit's interior. Both engines sounded smooth and clear to his practised ear; after a moment, Aschenbrenner checked each man at his station via the intercom. All checks completed, he finally called out, 'Stand by for take-off.'

The ground crew removed the wheel chocks, and pilot Aschenbrenner revved the engines to begin taxiing into take-off position. When the Heinkel reached its appointed stop on the airfield, where the wind blew straight down the aircraft's 'throat', he stepped on the brakes and waited. A Very flare arched into the air like a small, blazing comet, fired by a staff officer on the control tower, the token that Hauptmann Aschenbrenner had been waiting for, the signal that the bombing mission had begun. Aschenbrenner released the brakes and pushed the throttles forward; the Heinkel began rolling, slowly at first but then faster and faster until the ground rushed by in a continuous blur. Aschenbrenner hauled back on the controls when the ground speed indicator showed 130 mph and the bomber was airborne.

As the Heinkel climbed, after the undercarriage had been retracted, the navigator set a course for the Cherbourg Peninsula. Here the He111 would intercept radio beam 'Anton' and follow it to the target. Behind Aschenbrenner's aircraft, the other nineteen He111s of KG100 were now also taxiing into the wind, executing a climbing turn and setting out for Cherbourg. They reached their assigned altitude, 6,000 feet, and, one by one, the twenty Heinkels winged their way on a north-easterly line.

Hauptmann Aschenbrenner maintained a steady ground speed of 180 mph over cloud covered Brittany. Although the book claimed that the Heinkel's maximum speed, with bomb load, was 202 mph, this was laughingly dismissed by all who flew these bombers as either propaganda or just plain wishful thinking. Most He111s could do little better than 160 mph. Aschenbrenner's He111 H2 could fly slightly faster only because KG100 had engine overhauls more often than most bomb groups. At 180 mph, Aschenbrenner arrived over Cherbourg at 6.20, fifty minutes after take-off — right on time. The radioman signalled when they had locked onto X-beam 'Anton', and gave his pilot instructions to correct his course heading. On their present course and speed, Aschenbrenner would be over the City of London in 48 minutes, at 6.08 London time.

(*Right*) Sub-Officer Frederick Offord, of Redcross Street Fire Station.

(*Below*) 'On the end of a 100-foot ladder.' A fireman on a turntable ladder in the City, in a photo taken during an earlier raid on London.

# CHAPTER THREE

# 'Nothing to Report'
## *Late Afternoon – Evening*

In the Fire Service, things always seemed to go in extremes. The firemen were either bored senseless, or else rushed and harassed. There never seemed to be a happy medium.

The routine was the same at every fire station: at Holloway, in North London; Fire Brigade Headquarters, on the River in Lambeth; or at any of the fire houses throughout London. At Redcross Street Station, in the City, the Sunday papers had been read and disposed of long before. Most of the firemen occupied themselves by keeping equipment ready for a fire call. Sub-Officer Frederick Offord spent his weekly two-hour 'short leave' tidying up his gear and just pottering about.

Because of the long, dull daily routine, the Fire Brigade used to recruit largely from among ex-navy men. Life aboard ship was considered good practice for spending long, monotonous hours with only the same few faces. Firemen's jargon was filled with bits of naval lingo, even though most of the wartime men were civilian volunteers. When the floor needed a wash, the crew was ordered to 'scrub the deck'. The men were assembled with a shout of 'All hands on deck!' Even the LFB's slogan, which was worn on their helmets in pre-war days, was 'Ready Aye Ready'.

With the outbreak of war, recruits were taken from all walks of life. Sub-Officer Richard B. Horne's crew was typical. Horne was himself regular London Fire Brigade, but his men were all Auxiliary Fire Service volunteers: taxi drivers, manual labourers, clerks, a school teacher. They were all ready and willing, but largely untested and untrained in actual fire fighting.

The tedium was an ingrained part of the job to the regulars of the Fire Brigade, but most of the newcomers still had not adjusted to it. Edward Kelcey, serving with the Auxiliary Fire Service in Barnes, south-west London, had been sweeping, polishing brass, and looking at the four walls since morning. It was now late afternoon, and he was feeling restless and pent-up. He was also unhappy that he and his crew had been put on 'second turn-out', meaning that they were on stand-by status. Kelcey asked, and was granted, permission to be re-assigned to 'first turn-out' — in case of an alarm, he wanted to be the first one sent out.

A good many young men joined the Auxiliary Fire Service to avoid serving in the army, navy, or air force. After they were in, however, many of the auxiliaries found that they might have preferred the tender ministrations of a drill sergeant to their treatment by the regulars of the London Fire Brigade. Most of the 'old line' professional firemen were ex-servicemen, especially ex-naval officers, with a serviceman's reverence for strict discipline and spit-and-polish. They regarded the auxiliaries as totally unnecessary part-time firemen and, out of jealousy and pure vindictiveness, made life as uncomfortable as possible for the newcomers. In one instance, the regular LFB men refused to allow the auxiliaries to use their shower-baths, even after returning from a fire covered with filth and grime.

The firemen were not the only ones who were bored this afternoon. Special Constable R.E. Crowfoot had been on duty since 7.00 a.m. The City had been more than quiet all day, like it was every Sunday, and his shift had been slow and uneventful. During the afternoon, he dropped in on the firemen at Redcross Street Station for a chat, which had been one of the high points of his day.

When Constable Crowfoot's duty ended at 3.00, he reported back to Moor Lane Police Station to sign off, summing up his activities with a note, 'nothing to report'. After signing out, he left the City to spend the rest of his birthday with his elder brother at Stoke Newington, in North London.

With the day rapidly coming to a close, many Londoners, anticipating another raid-free night, were looking forward to a quiet Sunday evening. Across the river in Southwark, Edith Stannet waited for her husband, also a reserve constable, to come home from work. In Hornsey, north London, E.R. Cooke planned to spend a quiet evening with his parents. Vera Paxton was preparing for a date with an airman in Croydon, Surrey.

The long day that was just winding down for so many was only just beginning for Denys Tuckett. It was nearly dark when he arrived for work at the *Times* building on Queen Victoria Street, to begin preparing Monday morning's edition.

The staff of *The Times* no longer had to worry about retreating to the air raid shelter when the sirens sounded. The newspaper had been published from the old composing room for the past three months, well below ground. Ever since the *Times* building had been badly damaged by bombs late in September, the staff had been forced to work in the building's basement.

Even on the night of the bombing, the newspaper went to press on time. That edition failed to mention the damage to the building and, characteristically, did not even carry the story of its own adventure. From the large, single room, production went ahead as it had always done and the solid, dependable *Times* never missed an issue, regardless of enemy action.

Before they had even crossed the French coast, the twenty Heinkel He111s of Kampf Gruppe 100 were already registering on the radar screens of Britain's chain home stations. At Ventnor Station, on the Isle of Wight, the 300 foot steel masts picked up Hauptmann Friedrich Aschenbrenner's bombers while flying over the Gulf of St Malo, prior to their locking into X-beam 'Anton'. The glass radar screen inside Ventnor's receiver block came to life at about 5.15, as V-shaped blips of light, radio echoes of the approaching Heinkels, swam onto the tube. Almost immediately afterward, the WAAFs on duty reported this activity to Fighter Command Headquarters at Stanmore, Middlesex. 'Hello, Stanmore', the young woman's voice coolly informed, 'I have a plot of five − plus hostiles.' Five plus soon became ten plus and, as the Heinkels came into range one by one, finally reached a total of twenty.

At Stanmore − the Filter Room of Headquarters, Fighter Command at Bentley Priory, Stanmore, Middlesex, north-west of London − the radar plots were checked against any reports from other radar stations, and this screened data was then passed from the Filter Room to the adjacent Operations Room. The WAAFs on duty in the Operations Room next posted these contacts on a huge table map of England, which was as wide and long as a good sized sitting room. As the readings continued to come in from Ventnor, red metal arrows, representing the flight of hostile air-craft, were manoeuvred into position by a team of WAAFs using long, magnet-tipped plotting rods; as the aircraft advanced on their course, the red arrows were moved forward accordingly.

While the WAAFs were busy with their plots, the Operations Duty Controller relayed the radar sighting to Headquarters, Number 11 Fighter Group at Uxbridge, Middlesex. Number 11 Group was responsible for the protection of south-eastern England, including London, from air attack. After hearing from Stanmore, Headquarters 11 Group advised its sector airfields — aerodromes such as Tangmere, in West Sussex; Kenley, in Surrey; and Gravesend, Kent, which sent up fighters to patrol smaller sections of No 11 Group's territory — to stand by. Although this procedure may have been complex, it was also highly organised; the average elapsed time between Ventnor's initial contact and the ringing of the telephone in Tangmere's operations room spanned only six minutes, from first to last.

From Ventnor's Receiver Block, the plots were continually being read out. 'Hostile 20 at 100 miles. Height 6,000 feet. Range decreasing rapidly. Let us give you a bearing on that . . .'

Stanmore continued tracking the course of the hostiles; the red arrows pointed a steady north-easterly route. At this point the Duty Controller rang up his superior, Air Marshal Sholto Douglas, informing the Commander-in-Chief that 'something was on' for tonight. It looked like London again, but it was still too early to be sure. The only problem was with the height — 6,000 feet was abnormally low. Probably it was a mistake; Ventnor must surely mean 16,000 feet. The Controller snapped out an order: 'That height must be wrong. Tell Ventnor to check it.' But it was not a mistake. The WAAF wearing the unwieldy head-and-breast micro-phone and headset unit dully and methodically repeated the data from Ventnor radar. 'Hostile 20 at 6,000 feet. Range 75 miles and decreasing rapidly'. Aschenbrenner was flying only 1,500 feet above the clouds.

The red arrows kept on with their journey across the face of the great map, maintaining a bold, undeviating line toward the Sussex

At Gravesend, Kent, 'the young pilots of 85 Squadron climbed aboard their Hurricane fighters and coaxed their engines to life.' 85 Squadron's emblem, a white hexagon, is plainly visible.

'From their overhead gallery, the Operations Staff watched . . .' A flight of enemy bombers being plotted at Fighter Command Headquarters, Stanmore, Middlesex. Trafford Leigh-Mallory, with moustache, can be seen at the centre of the gallery.

coast. When the intruders passed beyond the arc of Ventnor's radar, the Observer Corps' posts in Sussex and Surrey normally continued to keep Stanmore informed, supplying visual fixes on the incoming aircraft. But tonight the ground observers could see nothing — the clouds successfully blocked out every trace of the raiders except for the steady drum-drum-drumming of their twin engines. All Stanmore could do was wait and hope for some concrete trace of the low-flying enemy airplanes.

By 5.15 p.m. the sky was almost totally dark. People all over London began preparing for another night in their air raid shelters, the 114th such night since the Blitz had begun.

Eileen Waterman and her father had just returned to their flat on Roscoe Street, half a mile to the north of St Paul's Cathedral. They had been out all day, and both were wearing their best Sunday clothes; before going down to their shelter, Eileen and her father changed from Sunday finery to 'shelter clothes'.

Over in Southwark, on the south bank of the Thames, Joy Hadfield was going through the same ritual. Just as she did every night, Miss Hadfield put on her old dungarees and descended into her family shelter.

By November, only 40% of Londoners slept in air raid shelters every night. The Luftwaffe had been limiting their visits to several nights per week instead of their previous nightly runs. The usual practice by that time was to wait until the sirens sounded before going to shelter.

Of this 40%, an estimated 27% used domestic shelters, retreating to their basement or back garden Anderson Shelter. An Anderson shelter consisted of a square hole dug in the ground, covered by two large U-shaped pieces of corrugated steel protruding above ground. The assembled shelter resembled a quonset hut, only much smaller. Surprisingly enough, most people found their Anderson shelter quite comfortable.

Nine per cent of London's population spent their nights in public shelters. These were usually in the basement of some large office building or factory, within easy walking distance of home. The air in these places tended to grow stale rather quickly, but aside from this drawback they were dry and warm.

One place that turned its basement into a public shelter was Thexton and Wright's, a clothing firm in Moorgate, in the City, which was now engaged in making uniforms for the army. Well over one hundred people slept here every night. The shelter featured a canteen, which was run by Mrs Craddock, a Thexton and Wright's employee. To keep costs to a minimum, Mrs Craddock cooked both breakfast and dinner for the residents, often putting in a sixteen hour day to keep the canteen going.

There was another kind of public shelter: square, squat, brick and cement cubicles called Pavement Shelters. The government built most of these during the earliest days of the war, and these could be seen dotting the pavement throughout London. These vaults were probably safe enough, but were very unpopular and usually deserted. Not only were they damp and draughty but, because they were right on the surface, they tended to absorb noise. During an air raid, there was plenty of noise to be absorbed. The bursting bombs were bad enough, but worse yet was the incessant blasting of the anti-aircraft guns, which made the walls rattle.

The most unsanitary shelters, and usually the most crowded, were the station platforms of the London Underground. On nights when an alert was on, the stations were mobbed with people. Some of the train stops had cots or bunks installed, but most people brought their bedding with them and slept on the cement platform. People sprawled all over the station platforms, making it difficult for passengers alighting from trains to avoid stepping on sleeping bodies. During severe air raids, they even curled up on the platform steps.

The living conditions in the tube stations were far from antiseptic. There was no means of washing. Shelterers usually wore the same clothes they had slept in last night. The lice and flea population was multiplying at an alarming rate. Doctors were becoming concerned about a possible epidemic of spotted fever and typhoid. 1940—41 was the cycle year for influenza; 'shelter cough' was a common sound in most Underground stations.

There was little privacy. Families tended to stay huddled closely together, always under the eyes of one another — and every other nearby family. The interruption of family life is graphically pointed out by the dramatic decline in the birth rate. During the week of 16th November, 378 births were recorded throughout London, as opposed to 1,070 in peacetime.

The stench was appalling. The fast trains, which were the closest thing to an efficient ventilation system now that the stations were used as living quarters, at least kept the air moving. After the trains stopped at 10 p.m. the atmosphere became increasingly foetid; when a latrine overflowed, the stench became unbearable. Workers entering the stations in the morning were nauseated by the smell. Some people walked or took the bus rather than endure the assault of foul air as they stepped off the street into the station.

The beginning of the Blitz in September introduced a new racket: the selling of shelter space. An enterprising fellow would arrive early at his chosen station and plant bundles of rags, which looked like bedding, at dozens of sleeping places. When evening came, he would approach a likely looking customer with, 'I'm supposed to hold this spot for a friend of mine, mister, but I'll give it to you instead — for a few shillings.' Rates varied, depending upon the size, facilities, and location of the shelter. In the deep and relatively clean West End Tube stations, like Oxford Circus and Green Park, prices started at two shillings and sixpence, only slightly less than for a good hotel room.

On this last Sunday before the New Year, the public shelters were already beginning to fill up. By now, the 'regulars' went more out of habit than the fear of bombs. They had been going to the same shelters for almost four months, and had struck up fast friendships within their miniature societies. Some had slept in the same spot for weeks on end, and felt that they were expected. Others were afraid that if they failed to show up, they might find someone else in their place the next time they needed it.

After more than 100 nights of the Blitz, the shelter routine was partly habit and partly instinct. Everyone had their own special way of moving to their nighttime residences. Some people simply picked up all their bedding and marched into the basement. A woman in Southwark moved into the darkest corner of her cellar, plugged her ears with cotton wool, and pulled the blankets over her head.

The Bayliss family, caretakers of an office building at London Wall near Finsbury Circus, had a somewhat more complex ritual. First, their menagerie of one dog, one cat, and a bird had to be taken care of. These were fed and watered and locked in separate offices until morning. Then the sandwiches had to be made and cut. Finally, Mrs Bayliss would put her mind at rest by storing her jewellery and trinkets in what she considered the safest place in the building — her kitchen oven.

It was nearly blackout time, 5.26 p.m., when the bells of St Bride's Church on Fleet Street chimed out their closing hymn, a New Year canticle saluting the passing year and hopefully anticipating the one to come. The playing of the hymn, the last one to be heard at St Bride's for seventeen years, marked the end of services. The parishioners, between thirty and forty people, walked out into the street and disappeared in the darkness.

Hauptmann Friedrich Aschenbrenner crossed the English coast at 5.47, according to the clocks in Sussex — right on time. Now that KG100 was beyond the scope of Ventnor's huge radar masts, flying inland 'behind' the coastal tracking stations, Fighter Command was now forced to rely upon the Observer Corps to track the intruding bomber force. The reports from the observers' posts were sketchy and ill-defined, however. This was not the fault of the men on duty who could not get even a glimpse of the Heinkels, and had no choice but to rely upon the sound of the bombers' engines in order to get some sort of plot. But an auditory fix was imprecise under the best of circumstances. The Heinkels' engines were deliberately out of synchronisation to confuse the Observer Corps' sound detection apparatus, making plotting by ear even more vague and inaccurate.

At Number 11 Group Headquarters in Uxbridge, Middlesex, Sir Trafford Leigh-Mallory, the Group's Commanding Officer, already had enough information. The enemy bombers would be winging their way across West Sussex, well within the radius of Tangmere Air Station's sector, whatever their destination. The Operations Controller was ordered to ring up Tangmere and alert 219 Beaufighter Squadron, scrambling the night-fighters into position high above the reaches of Sussex.

During the Battle of Britain, 219 Squadron had been stationed near Newcastle-upon-Tyne, close by the Scottish border, where it had flown single-engined and generally inadequate Bristol Blenheim fighters. Since the nightly Blitz began, the squadron was moved to Tangmere, bag and baggage, and equipped with the twin-engined Beaufighters. Not only were the Beaufighters faster and more manoeuverable than the Blenheims, but had a fuel capacity that allowed each fighter to remain in the air for hours, and boasted a devastating firepower from four 20 mm cannon and six .303 Browning machine guns. The most remarkable feature of 219's Squadron's Beaufighters, however, was their new airborne radar sets, the AI Mark IV.

The AI radar enabled the Beaufighter's two-man crew to intercept enemy raiders despite the cover of darkness; the Mark IV sets were the newest and most reliable version. When a hostile aircraft crossed the coast, the Beaufighter was brought into position by a ground controller until the pursuit ship's own radar was close enough to pick up the enemy. The night-fighter's two-man pilot-observer team then followed the electric blip on the AI screen until the enemy was within visual distance. At that point the pilot took over, closing stealthily toward the dark, looming bomber until it crowded the ring of his gunsight. The range between the Beaufighter and its unsuspecting prey would be about 100 yards when the pilot pressed the firing button; the four cannon and six machine guns in the Beaufighter's nose would quickly send the enemy aircraft plunging earthward in a blaze of exploding gasoline.

This is what happened in an ideal combat. Usually, however, there were few contacts and even fewer confirmed kills. At the height of the Blitz in mid-September, from the 19th to the 23rd, over 160 night-fighter sorties were flown against the Luftwaffe's bomber forces attacking London. Of these 160-odd flights, one fighter claimed an interception — but no kill, just an interception. Since September, the record of the night-fighters did show some improvement, but the Luftwaffe's Air Fleets still ranged over England, largely unmolested.

The shortcomings of the AI airborne radar were largely at fault for the lack of enemy contacts; it was still new and having more than its share of teething pains. Often the vibration of the Beau-fighters' twin engines would be enough to knock out the sensitive radar set. The set would function beautifully on the ground, but when switched on in the air — nothing. The blast of the night-fighter's ten guns could also render the radar inoperable. And if the target aircraft saw the Beaufighter moving into firing position and banked steeply away, the AI set would never find its target again.

Filled with hope but far from optimistic, the two-man crews of 219 Beaufighter Squadron lifted off from Tangmere's runway to try their luck. Their assigned altitude was above 12,000 feet — the maximum effective height of anti-aircraft fire — although pilots often went below this altitude when pursuing an intruding Heinkel or a swift winged Junkers bomber.

Even though 219 Squadron had almost no hope at all of spotting the twenty He111s of Kampf Gruppe 100, since they would be flying 6,000 feet above the 'Fire Raisers', it might not be an uneventful night for them after all. Across the Channel in northern France, slightly over an hour's flying time for the speedy Beaufighters, the gloomy winter twilight was being shattered by the roaring engines of Luftwaffe bomber squadrons preparing for their strike against London. The first units were already being picked up by British Chain Home stations at Pevensey, Rye, and Swinggate on the Kentish coast, as well as Ventnor, and their radar plots relayed instantly to Stanmore. The great table map of England was aglow with red arrows; WAAFs listened intently to the reports coming in from the south coast. This was no small raid, as it had first appeared. It was clear to Air Marshal Sholto Douglas that something out of the ordinary was taking shape.

The instinct to 'go underground' went a step further in some of London's residents. The insistence by foreign news reporters that Londoners had developed a sixth sense about air raids, that they could tell by intuition when a bad one was coming, was given some foundation this night. Many more people than usual shunned the protection of their basements and made for the deep shelters. Underground stations were packed, more crowded than they had been in weeks. Shelterers filled the platforms, leaving only narrow passageways open for the passengers, and spilled over on to the exit stairs.

This sense was not limited to civilians. At Whitefriars Fire Station, based at King's College on the Strand, a senior Fire Brigade officer dropped in while making his rounds of the district. He told Station Officer Laurence J. Odling he had a feeling 'that we are going to get it tonight'.

Six thousand feet above the countryside of Surrey, Hauptmann Friedrich Aschenbrenner held firmly to the controls of his He111 H2, pointing the aircraft directly toward Central London. Beneath the roaring bomber, a carpet of fleecy grey carpet stretched as far as the eye could see, concealing the blacked-out towns below from sight. For all Aschenbrenner knew, he might be anywhere, miles off course. But his radio operator knew that they were precisely on course; the steady, uniform sound made by X-beam 'Anton' registering in his headset guided him as clearly as a homing flare path.

When the aircraft reached Mitcham, Surrey, the tone of the X-beam changed abruptly to a series of buzzing throbs — the 'advance signal' had been reached. The radioman purposefully reached over and started the X-apparatus' electric timer, setting in motion the automatic sequence of events which would climax in the dropping of 288 incendiary bombs. Aschenbrenner was now obliged to maintain an exacting flight path — no variation in either course, speed, or height would be allowed for the next three minutes. Any alteration from this straight course would confuse the X-apparatus, rendering it useless and ruining the bomb run. Until they reached their target, Aschenbrenner and his crewmen would be like clay targets in a skeet shoot. They had no idea that there were any British night fighters up, which was just as well since they would not be able to evade them. If the Beaufighters of 219 Squadron spotted them now, there would be no chance to escape.

The first people in London who knew that something definitely was 'on' for tonight were Commander Aylmer Firebrace, the London Fire Brigade's Chief of Fire Staff, and his Senior Staff

'A tall, ruddy-complexioned man . . .' Commander Aylmer Firebrace, Regional Fire Officer attached to the Home Office, who made the 'tour of the fires'.

Officer, A.P.L. Sullivan. At a very few minutes before 6.00 p.m. a telephone call from Air Marshal Sholto Douglas' Operations Room at Stanmore, Middlesex came through to the Home Office Fire Control Room, which was in Whitehall, a few minutes walk from the Houses of Parliament. The word was that a German bomber formation — larger than usual — had been picked up on radar, and was being tracked on its approach from the south. The attacking force was following a heading that would take it straight to London.

# CHAPTER FOUR

# 'The Third One is Never Like the Rest'
## *6pm – 6.30pm*

Charles Sone left his house in Southwark a few minutes before 6.00 p.m., as he did every night, on his way to Upper Thames Street in the City district. At six o'clock he was slated to begin his shift at the Civil Defence Control Centre. As he crossed the River Thames over Southwark Bridge, Sone could hear the droning of aeroplane engines.

A short distance away, near St George's Circus in Southwark, eighteen year-old Joy Hadfield also heard the approaching aircraft. The buzzing throb of the engines, out of synchronisation to confuse anti-aircraft tracking equipment, told her at once that they were not 'ours'. One plane in particular bothered her – probably Hauptmann Aschenbrenner's Heinkel, which flew almost directly over St George's Circus. Its motors must have been further out of tune than the others; to Miss Hadfield, it sounded like 'a great dirty bee'.

In their flat at Number 34 Lime Street, Mrs Ivy Ing and her husband could not hear the converging aircraft but the air raid alert was clear enough. Their air raid shelter was only a few doors away, in the basement of an office building at Number 38 Lime Street. When the sirens sounded, they both walked down the seven flights of stairs to the street and headed straight for it.

Kampf Gruppe 100's twenty Heinkel bombers kept to their straight, unwavering flight path, droning over south London at a steady three miles per minute. In the leading bomber, Hauptmann Friedrich Aschenbrenner held the controls with a light but sure touch; from the compartment behind the pilot, the radio operator kept both ears tuned to his headset. Over two minutes had gone since the X-beam's 'advance signal' had been passed, but as the Heinkel's twin engines growled monotonously over

Kennington the watchful bomb-aimer and the two gunners could see no signs of life. They could see nothing at all, in fact, except solid cloud.

Then the radioman put both hands in his earphones and stiffened. The tone of the radio beam had once again changed suddenly as the aircraft passed through the 'main signal' — Aschenbrenner and his crew were directly over the target. The radio operator tersely announced their arrival via the intercom; a second later, the bomb-aimer, at the ready, pressed the bomb release. Eight canisters of incendiaries fell out of the bomb bay toward the layers of cloud 1,500 feet below. The bomb aimer, his voice edged with tenseness, announced 'Bombs gone!' into his microphone.

The eight 'Molotov Breadbaskets' plunged through the clouds and continued plummeting for about another thirty seconds. When they were about one thousand feet above the ground, the canisters, one by one, broke open and spilled their contents over a radius of a few hundred yards. The foot-long incendiaries came to rest with a metallic *craack* and a glittering shower of magnesium — in Southwark, just south of the Thames. Hauptmann Aschenbrenner had missed his target, the City of London, by about 1,000 yards.

As soon as he heard 'Bombs gone!' Aschenbrenner gave the Heinkel some rudder and, while everyone breathed a sigh of relief, turned off the flight path and began to climb. He continued his climbing turn until the aircraft was several thousand feet above bombing altitude, when he levelled off and started cruising in a wide circle. Hauptmann Aschenbrenner, as commander of KG100, now took up a position where he could observe the efforts of his élite bombing wing and watch the results of their labours.

The attacking bomber force arrived overhead with much less warning than during any past air raid. Veteran fire watching crews who had been involved in many bombings since the Blitz had begun were caught off guard by the swiftness of tonight's attack. At St Paul's Cathedral one of the men on roof patrol phoned the Cathedral control centre at 6.05, reporting that air raid sirens were sounding out to the south-west. George Garwood received the call and, after hearing the report, told the patrol that he would be right with him. Before Garwood could put on his axe belt and helmet, the patrol phoned again — he could see incendiary bombs falling across the river in Southwark. The local sirens were now sounding; by the time Garwood reached the roof, fire bombs were dropping on the Cathedral itself.

Olive Bayliss, living with her family at London Wall near Finsbury Circus, was certain that the raiders came in faster than usual tonight. At any rate, they were overhead before the usual shelter preparations could be completed, catching everyone by surprise. Olive's father, an Air Raid Warden, lost no time in clearing the flat when the first fire bombs clattered on the roof, calmly telling Olive and her mother, 'All right, we'd better get out of the way.' Before he went down to the shelter himself, Mr Bayliss climbed up on the roof to extinguish the bombs that had landed.

At Redcross Street Fire Station, Fireman James Goldsmith's dull and boring day came to an abrupt end. When the sirens went, his stomach muscles involuntarily tensed up as he thought, 'Here we go again!'

When the two-pound bombs began to fall, most people reacted calmly and methodically to the danger. Mrs C. Smokes, who was spending the night in the deep shelter at London Bridge with her parents, was out walking with some friends when the attack began. They heard the air raid sirens, but there didn't seem to be much happening so they kept on walking. Before they got very far, bursting fire bombs began to jump out of the darkness all round them. The group decided, calmly but hastily, that they had better get back to the shelter.

For those so inclined, the bursting fire bombs, dancing vividly to life in the blacked-out streets, were a pleasure to watch. It was hard to imagine that the bright sparklers, looking like so many Christmas crackers, were capable of doing damage. The large, ugly 550 lb high-explosive bombs, generating vicious blast waves in all directions, were a different matter.

The blast from these bombs had a psychological, almost supernatural, aspect that went far beyond their capabilities for physical destruction. Shock waves could derail a train or wrench the steering wheel right out of a bus driver's grasp, as though an evil hand had come out of nowhere to wreak havoc among the unsuspecting. Sometimes a bursting bomb seemed to have the unearthly power of choosing its victims, killing a man a hundred yards away yet sparing someone standing almost on top of the explosion.

Streets concealing underground pipes and cables were torn up, disrupting not only vital defence communications but also cutting off water and power for everyday life. The dead from cemeteries were heaved up out of their graves, the blast strewing bones and remains of corpses for hundreds of yards. Violent and immediate was the impact of a high-explosive bomb. But the little two-pound incendiaries seemed more appropriate in a children's pageant than in an air raid. They looked totally out of place in their role as agents of fire and destruction.

Even though the attack was only a few minutes old, some had a presentiment that tonight's bombing was not going to be just another small 'nuisance' raid. Fire watcher Leonard Atkinson had arrived at Blackfriars shortly before six o'clock, on his way to his firm, a building society on Ludgate Hill, for roof-spotting duties. During the short walk to his post, the back streets were peppered by a torrent of fire bombs which lit the roadway and pavement all around with glittering white furies. It was obvious to him that this was the beginning of a bad raid.

When the incendiary clusters began pelting the vicinity of the ancient, gable-roofed Guildhall Mr F.A. George, Commander of Guildhall's Fire Squad Number 2, made certain that all fire watcher's posts were manned immediately. Within minutes, his foresight paid off. Shortly after the alert, the patrols reported a number of fire bombs on Guildhall's roofs, and went to work extinguishing them at once.

In her air raid shelter in the basement of Number 38 Lime Street, Mrs Ivy Ing overheard someone say that this was sure to be a very serious attack. It was the third time in a week that the sirens had sounded, a very bad omen since 'the third one is never like the rest'.

Not every fire bomb posed an immediate threat. Some failed to ignite, landing on the pavement with a dull, plopping sound. Five bombs landed on the newspaper offices of Bouverie House in Fleet Street. Of the five, one did not explode, one burnt itself out

"Fires were already out of control and spreading." Within only a few minutes after the air raid began, the two-foot long magnesium bombs had already started several large fires within the City.

Incendiaries bursting in a London street, '. . . a glittering shower of white, molten splinters.' Note the white painted stripes on the lampposts, for visibility in the black-out.

on the concrete roof, and the other three were extinguished by the night watchman.

The fire watchers at St Paul's Cathedral were deluged by a hail of incendiaries. The IBs were giving the men some trouble, but nothing they could not handle. The main problem was with the Cathedral's 'double-boarded' roofs, a system of two-layered ceilings made up of a lead-covered outer roof and, a few feet below, a wooden inner roof. The two-pound bombs were just heavy enough to punch through the lead covering of the outer roof and penetrate inside. The impact of a falling bomb would simply cut out a lead disc about the size of a half-crown and break through the wood underneath. Sputtering violently, the bomb would lodge itself in the space between the two roofs. There, an incendiary could start a very hot fire in a remarkably short time.

Shortly after the 'red' alert came through, an incendiary pierced one of the main roofs and started a small fire. Fortunately, the fire was discovered early, but extinguishing the blaze would not be as simple as finding it. Because the smouldering bomb was so hard to reach, wedged into a small space between the double roof, and because the 260 year-old roof timbers burned so easily, the small fire threatened to spread. But the flames were assaulted right away by George Garwood and his partner Mr Ben Burrows. Tackling the blaze from above and below with a stirrup pump — a hand pump fed by a bucket of water — the pair soon had it extinguished.

The other nineteen Heinkels of Kampf Gruppe 100 enjoyed somewhat better accuracy than their leader, Hauptmann Friedrich Aschenbrenner. The bombers flew in precise single file, nose-to-tail, following the tone of X-beam 'Anton' to the target area; as each aircraft passed the 'main signal', the bomb-aimer toggled the canisters of incendiaries. Although Aschenbrenner had missed the City by a scant 1,000 yards — no mean feat, considering that he could not even see the ground — most of the other crews managed to put their bombs right on target, with a little luck and the help of a slight north-easterly wind. No one knew precisely where their bombs were going, anymore than Aschenbrenner did, because of the dense overcast sky. Everyone just unloaded automatically where the X-beams crossed.

It was clear by this time that London had come to life. Batteries of searchlights were doing their best to pick out the intruders, but the bomber crews could not see these — the beams of light were eaten up by the thick cloud cover. But the anti-aircraft fire was plain enough. Bright red — orange globes burst through the clouds, rising gracefully past the speeding aircraft like glowing neon bubbles, and exploded harmlessly somewhere overhead. The flak was distracting enough to make everybody look, but not close enough to disrupt their bomb run.

One by one, the twin-engined He111s reached the 'main signal', dropped their bombs, turned, and set their course for home base in Vannes, Brittany. Only Hauptmann Aschenbrenner remained behind. Aschenbrenner orbited slowly over the target area, above 12,000 feet and well out of anti-aircraft range, observing his men drop their firebombs with the calmness of a theatre-goer watching a well-rehearsed but none too interesting play.

The atmosphere inside the Operations Room at Fighter Command Headquarters, Stanmore, also was quiet, but here the tranquillity masked a growing tenseness. Radar plots from the coastal Chain Home stations were still coming in at a steady rate: Pevensey was plotting 15 hostiles just crossing the Kentish coast; Rye had another 20 plus still over France. The WAAFs deftly wielded their long, magnet-tipped plotting rods, manoeuvering an increasing number of red arrows across the great table map, keeping both ears tuned for fresh plots from the south coast.

In the Controller's Gallery above the map table, Air Marshal Sholto Douglas and his staff took in the scene below. The Air Marshal had a battery of telephones at his finger-tips — one to the Home Office, one to Fire Brigade Headquarters in Lambeth, one to Anti-Aircraft Command — all of which had been used during the past half hour. His Operations Officer had notified every department of the air raid's progress, from the government offices in Whitehall and the RAF airfields to Air Raid Warden's posts and police stations. Having done all this, Douglas and his officers could now do nothing except stand on their balcony and watch as the WAAFs below monitored the positions of the incoming raiders. More and more arrows were appearing on the map's face; each one pointed straight at London.

At Lloyds Bank Buildings, 55/61 Moorgate, the fire watchers were as busy as the men at St Paul's, dousing incendiaries before they could do any damage. Down below, Doris Walsby had her own duties. While her husband and the rest of the crew were up on the roof, she and her daughter set themselves to making 'endless cups of tea'.

Edith Stannet and her husband, in their small coffee shop in back of Guy's Hospital, Southwark, were kept busy doing the same thing as Mrs Walsby, but on a grander scale. Mrs Stannet's husband, a City of London Reserve Constable, had just come off duty when they heard the sirens. They were both about to dash off to their nearby air raid shelter, in the basement of a leather goods warehouse, when Mrs Stannet heard the 'swishing noise' of a falling Molotov Breadbasket followed by 'fires in all directions'.

She could see that a bad night was in store, and knew from past experience that firemen would be dropping in for hot drinks all through it. Mrs Stannet turned around and went back into her kitchen, banked up the old coal stove, and began filling all available pans and kettles with water.

This was the first time that so many incendiaries had been dropped on Central London; even the raids of September and October had not seen fire bombs in these quantities. Throughout the City, Southwark, and southern Islington (the district just north of the City boundary), people who were above ground saw and heard the same things: the clatter and crack of bombs striking the roadway and nearby buildings, followed immediately by a host of dazzling white sparklers leaping out of the darkness.

Visually, the effect was both startling and awe-inspiring. Everything took on a vaguely sinister aspect in the stark white light of the glittering bombs; even familiar buildings and streets looked different, unreal.

The few Air Raid Wardens and fire watchers on duty stared at the sight as if transfixed, held momentarily speechless by the scene. For every incendiary that spent itself in a gaudy show on pavements and rooftops, however, there was at least one bomb that pierced a slate or wood roof and glowed with equal fury — white-hot magnesium reached 4,000° F — among wooden beams or highly inflammable furnishings.

To Surgery Attendant Frank Wright, on duty at St Bartholo-mew's Hospital, the falling two-pound bombs seemed to come down like 'fish dumped out of a net'. Within the first few minutes of the raid, he saw fires spring up suddenly in scattered areas all over the City and Southwark. From the hospital roof, it was quite a spectacle.

St Bart's itself had been hit several times, but the bombs were extinguished before they could do any serious damage. One bomb embedded itself in the concrete outside the nurses' quarters. A second landed inside one of the surgical theatres, where it was taken care of by the staff.

Mrs Matthews, the wife of the Dean of St Paul's, could not see the bombs as they burst into a spray of molten splinters, but even from the Cathedral's crypt she could hear them hitting the roof. They reminded her of coal being spilled out of a scuttle. The fire watchers on the roofs could tell that actually there were several clusters falling in quick succession.

There were some who managed to avert their eyes from the bursting incendiaries and take note of other things. From a roof-top post at Stapley and Smith Ltd., a ladies clothing warehouse on Fore Street, firewatcher R.C.H. Constable was most of all im-pressed by the searchlight beams that probed the cloudy sky for the invisible raiders. At W & D Harvest, Spices and Sundries warehouse in Dowgate Dock, close by Cannon Street Railway Station, firewatcher Benjamin W. Davis was most impressed by what he did not perceive. The anti-aircraft guns had gone into their usual ear-shattering routine shortly after the sirens, and the fire bombs came down in an endless string of smacks and cracks. But one noise was missing from the usual din. The low, muffled *crrruummmp* of high explosive bombs was absent tonight.

Most people were too pre-occupied with their own problems to notice such details. Stanley G. Champion and his partner Howard had been watch at Jackson Brothers Ltd., at Number 47 Old Street, in Islington, since 4.00 p.m. When the sirens wailed their warning both men were in the basement; the alarm sent them running for their rooftop post. As they stepped outside on the roof, they were greeted by a storm of steel splinters from bursting anti-aircraft shells. The two had bolted from the basement in such a hurry that they had forgotten to put on their helmets, but the rain of shrapnel served as a nasty reminder. Champion and his partner retreated hastily to the cellar to retrieve their tin hats.

Mrs Eileen McConville was caught out in the open by the suddenness of Kampf Gruppe 100's attack. A telephone operator at the London Trunk Exchange, in the Faraday Building, Mrs McConville had only just come off duty at 6.00. She was crossing Blackfriars Bridge, on her way to Waterloo Railway Station and a train home; when she heard the air raid sirens, Mrs McConville paused for a moment. The eerie howl was followed immediately by the droning of aircraft, then flames seemed suddenly to spring up everywhere. Deciding that she had seen enough, and nearly deafened by the noise of the aircraft and the roaring bark of the anti-aircraft guns, Mrs McConville continued to press on toward Waterloo Station.

Waterloo, as well as nearly every rail station in and near Central London, would be the stopping-off point for a good many people tonight. Most of these visits, however, were unplanned and frequently were quite uncomfortable. Engine driver F. Whittle was taking his train through Vauxhall Station, about a mile to the south, when the alert sounded. He had no sooner reached Waterloo than the bombs began dropping, followed by a loud-speaker announcement that passengers and station personnel should take shelter in the Underground station. But Whittle did not want to leave his engine, and elected to take cover under the platform near his train. From there, he had a good view of the fires as they began to take hold.

Another recent arrival at Waterloo Station was Mrs Dorothy Johnson. Mrs Johnson was among tonight's unwilling visitors. She was on her way home to Catford, south-east London, after having spent a week visiting her husband at an RAF training station in northern England. Her train from the north had just reached Euston Railway Station, when the air raid sirens started up. Although she managed to get a taxi, the driver refused to take her to Catford during an attack. He turned Mrs Johnson out at Waterloo, abruptly telling her that she was on her own.

'The incendiaries were falling fast and furious,' Mrs Johnson recalls; the station, along with several trains and vehicles, was 'well and truly burning'. Frightened and thoroughly disoriented, Mrs Johnson paid the taxi driver and, looking for cover, ran behind a milk churn, then into a telephone coin box. After she was able to collect her thoughts, Mrs Johnson realised that a phone box, with all its glass, was not the place to be during an air raid. But with everyone dashing about in a panic and the station afire, she had no idea where she should go or what she was supposed to do.

Her distress was not helped any when a fire bomb hit the luggage of a nearby couple saying their farewells. The couple was not hurt but their suitcases were badly damaged, bursting into flames before their, and Mrs Johnson's, astonished eyes. Finally, an Air Raid Warden spotted her and, taking her in hand, led Mrs Johnson to the Underground shelter.

The fire crew at Guildhall did not need instructions. The men had smothered every fire bomb that fell on their ancient hall quickly and efficiently, much to the satisfaction of Commander F.A. George. At 6.25, Commander George ordered the sand and water buckets to be refilled, and sent an additional man to each post.

The efficiency of Guildhall's fire squad was exceptional. In scattered areas throughout the City, Islington, and Southwark, fires were already out of control and spreading. It had been only fifteen minutes since the raid had begun when H.A. Penny, at his house in Paddington, four miles to the west of the growing blaze, noted, 'I could see a very large fire over City way.'

Even as the last of Kampf Gruppe 100's Heinkels turned and headed toward Brittany, Hauptmann Friedrich Aschenbrenner still circled high above the target. Through the thick overcast Aschenbrenner could already see a dim red blush burning far below. His hand-picked pilots and air crews had done a thorough job, better than at Coventry; the brightly lit-up target area would serve as an indelible aiming point for the rest of Luftflotte 3. The fires which KG100 had set were clearly visible above 12,000 feet despite the cloud layer. Hauptmann Aschenbrenner instructed his radio operator to send a report to Generalfeldmarschall Hugo Sperrle at Air Fleet Three Headquarters in Paris: The target had been successfully bombed and fierce fires raged, while more bombers were on their way toward London.

Major Schulz-Hein, commanding I Wing of Kampfgeschwader 51, could see nothing from the cockpit of his Junkers Ju 88 except the stars above his aircraft and endless cloud and anti-aircraft bursts beneath. He had thought that tonight's raid was idiotic from the very outset; the longer he flew along his navigator's course, the more he thought so. It had been nearly half an hour since his Junkers had crossed the English coast. According to Schulz-Hein's calculations, he and his crew should now be approaching London. Only he could not see London or anything else except a floor of light grey that stretched in all directions. It was mad to have to fly a bombing mission under these conditions, the Major felt. He had about as much of a chance of bombing his target as he would of dropping a pebble into a hat from a rooftop while wearing a blindfold.

All at once Major Schulz-Hein looked hard at something up ahead, as a wanderer on the desert stares at a mirage. But his eyes were not playing tricks on him. Far below his hurtling aircraft, a rose-coloured translucent glow lit up a patch of cloud as if by magic. Schulz-Hein was looking at the same sight that Hauptmann Aschenbrenner had observed a few minutes before — the light of the spreading fires set by KG100 in the City of London and Southwark shining through the overcast. Major Schulz-Hein knew that he had found his target.

The fire bombs of Kampf Gruppe 100 had done their job thoroughly and with frightening efficiency, punching or burning their way through roofs to start hundreds of widespread combustions. These insignificant smoulderings had stoked themselves into major fires within an astonishingly short time.

It had still been quiet when M.S. Saunders left work at Solomon and Gluckstein, at Number 2/14 Exchange Street, and began his ten minute walk to his flat in Islington. The anti-aircraft fire started up when he reached home, but Saunders had no idea whether London was being attacked or if the raiders were just passing over on their way to another target. The general din continued all through his meal. After he had eaten, Saunders went up on the roof to see what was happening and discovered flames burning within the City.

# CHAPTER FIVE

# 'Now, Don't Tell me that you Don't See *them!*'
## *6.30pm — 7pm*

The anti-aircraft fire was as heavy as anyone had ever seen it, but not thick enough to intimidate Major Schulz-Hein of Kampf-geschwader 51. From the left-hand seat of his Junkers Ju88 cockpit, the Major gently manoeuvered the aircraft toward the lit-up section of cloud that marked the target area. The flak was not very accurate for all its volume, allowing the Major to take his time and make a good bombing run. And Schulz-Hein fully intended to take all the time he needed. He had been cursing this mission since early afternoon, but now that he had his target in sight, he was determined to put every one of the incendiaries in the bomb-bay dead on it.

Schulz-Hein's Junkers carried twelve canisters of fire bombs in its bomb racks — a grand total of 432 of the foot-long missiles. Some of KG51's Ju88s were loaded with a mix of incendiaries and 550 lb high-explosive bombs. The awkward quarter-ton cargoes of explosives, large, grim looking objects next to the thinner and rather plain Molotov Breadbaskets, were calculated to hinder London's firemen and generally create as much havoc as possible. As it turned out, the bombs more than accomplished their job.

In the forward section of the Junkers, the bomb-aimer, lying prone on his stomach, peered through the plexiglass nose. While sighting intently through the bomb aiming device, he silently manipulated a battery of dials and switches, minutely adjusting the apparatus. Although the target had been brightly illuminated by the 'Fire Raisers' of Kampf Gruppe 100, it would not be impossible to overshoot the mark; he did not come all this way just to miss. Carelessness or sloppy settings could ruin an otherwise perfect run-in.

The bomb-bay doors were open. Occasionally, the bomb-aimer would intone instructions to Major Schulz-Hein at the controls — 'Come right a few degrees. That's it. Now steady . . .' — but mostly he stared straight into the bomb sight, delicately fingering the adjusting dials. When he was satisfied that the aircraft was directly over the City of London the bomb-aimer pressed the release button, salvoeing the twelve bomb canisters into the night. 'Bombs Gone!' crackled in the headsets of the pilot and radioman, the voice brimming with relief.

Not many people noticed the few minutes' lull in the bombing between the departure of Kampf Gruppe 100 and the arrival of Kampfgeschwader 51 over the target. The aerial attack seemed like one endless onslaught to the fire watchers on duty within the target area; there was no time to observe minor details. It was about 6.30 when the first fire bombs fell on Old Street, just north of the City boundary. At Jackson Brothers Ltd., Number 47 Old Street, Stanley G. Champion and his partner Howard heard the familiar, disquieting noise made by falling Molotov Breadbaskets; a 'loud swishing sound, followed by light thuds'.

Champion and his partner, along with two men from Grosvenor Charters, the export stationer's and paper-makers at Number 51 Old Street, grabbed buckets of sand and dashed for the emergency exit. Several were sputtering furiously right outside the door. The four fire watchers snuffed them out by covering them with sand.

But the fire bombs seemed to hit everywhere at once. No sooner had this cluster been extinguished than Champion spotted a red glow coming from the top floor of a building at the end of the yard. He and his partner Howard took fire axes, ran across the yard to the burning building, and began knocking down the locked door. While they were busy chopping, someone noticed that Grosvenor Charters had been hit and that Jackson Brothers was also alight.

In an attempt to organise the chaos, the crew split into pairs. The two men from Grosvenor Charters headed for their building, while Stanley Champion and Howard ran back up the stairs of Jackson Brothers with a stirrup pump and buckets of water.

Howard burst through the doors as soon as he reached the top floor. He was met by a wall of fire. Howard and Champion could see that they were hardly a match for the blaze — this was no job for two men with a bucket of water. After a moment, Stanley Champion announced that he was going to run for the fire brigade. He charged down the stairs to the street and hurried toward the Auxiliary Fire Station in Baltic Street, about two hundred yards away.

Down on Ludgate Hill, Leonard Atkinson and his two partners were having their own troubles. They did not have any sand, and the fine spray from their stirrup pumps was useless. So they put out the bombs on the Building Society's roof the only way they could — by throwing an entire bucket of water over them, risking a violent explosion from the water hitting the white-hot magnesium.

Major Schulz-Hein and his two-man crew felt utterly satisfied with their performance. The bomb load had gone straight through the centre of the illuminated patch in the cloud layer; there was no chance at all that they could have missed, especially since their aiming point was the old and highly inflammable City district. The London Fire Brigade certainly would not get any sleep tonight.

With all bombs gone, there was nothing more to do except turn around and go home. The radio operator notified home base at Melun, just south of Paris, that the target had been bombed. The bomb-aimer, reverting back to his role of navigator, worked out a course back to their airfield. As they turned onto their homeward-bound heading, Major Schulz-Hein caught sight of other bombers, outlined in the russet shimmer of the fires far below, making their own run-in toward the target.

Although the incendiaries were dropping in a fast and steady stream, some people had to be convinced. Shortly after 6.30 a dispatch rider stood at the door of Redcross Street Fire Station, idly looking out at the buildings on Jewin Street. All of a sudden he announced that he had seen two incendiaries fall. No one else could see them, since they had penetrated the roof of one of the buildings and detonated inside. A few minutes later the same thing happened. Two more IBs fell, the man said. Again, everybody got up to look and, again, no one could see anything.

Shortly after this, three bombs fell directly outside the fire station, bursting into a fury of molten splinters as they struck the pavement. This time, everybody scrambled for sand to extinguish them. Before everyone was out of earshot, the dispatch rider shouted after them with self-satisfaction, 'Now, don't tell me that you don't see *them*!' During the next few hours, no one inside Redcross Street Station would have to be convinced of the fire bombs. The entire area surrounding the fire house would be a raging inferno.

Gordon Papps was standing his shift at the textile firm of Hitchcock, Williams & Co. Ltd., at Number 69/70 St Paul's Churchyard, only a few yards north of the Cathedral. As a member of the fire watch, Mr Papps was on and off the building's flat roof as his duties required. The entire Paternoster Square area was being pelted by a rain of incendiaries. The crew at Hitchcock, Williams quickly doused the IBs that fell on their building, but the surrounding factories and warehouses apparently had no roof watchers on duty and soon were blazing bonfires.

From the roof, Gordon Papps had a front row view of the rapidly spreading blaze. Papps was usually afraid of heights, and loathed roof duty, but tonight it was different. He found the fires strangely awe-inspiring. The sight of the field of raging red flames made him forget all about his nerves.

It did not take long before the surrounding buildings, old textile warehouses and book depositories with slate roofs and wooden interiors, were blazing beyond control. The stores of books were the first to go up in flames. Hot air all round made the books as dry as tinder; when the fires intensified, this concentrated heat cracked the glass in the windows. As hot air whooshed in through the broken panes, having a temperature of several hundred degrees, the row upon row of volumes burst into flame all at once, with explosive suddenness. Fires began to lick at Hitchcock, Williams & Co., and soon had the western end of the structure alight. Still exhilarated by the night's excitement, Gordon Papps eagerly tackled the combustion with a chemical fire extinguisher. He thought shooting the foam about was 'grand fun'.

The last time that this district burned was in 1666, during the Great Fire of London. Ivy Lane, Paul's Alley, Paternoster Row, and all of the quarter just north of Old St Paul's began burning on the third day of the fire. The area continued to blaze until there was nothing left but smoking, blackened ruins. The booksellers and textile merchants were hit hard by that fire as well, losing virtually all of their stock. What had taken days to destroy in 1666, however, was now being brought down in a matter of hours.

Just across the courtyard, the fire watch at St Paul's Cathedral were too preoccupied to take much notice of the spectacle all around them. Members of the part-time volunteer squad who lived nearby began to filter in by ones and twos, reinforcing the full-time crew. The volunteers were assigned to roof duty, leaving the regulars to inspect the inside of the great cathedral, with all its galleries and walkways.

The members of the St Paul's Watch managed to extinguish every fire before it could spread and get out of hand, but another hazard threatened the cathedral. St Paul's was now surrounded by burning buildings: on the north by Paternoster Square; on the east by the blazing office blocks of Old Change; and by the buildings of Carter Lane and the churchyard to the south. The flames were spreading and growing more fierce literally by the minute. Burning debris from these buildings blew right across the narrow church-yard and lighted on the cathedral; the roof of the choir soon became perilously hot. The Cathedral Watch now had another duty — walking around the roof with wet sacks, putting out the sparks.

The cascade of two-foot long bombs showed no sign of letting up. The fire watchers on the roof of the *Daily Telegraph* Building in Fleet Street had a full view of St Paul's from the west, and reported that a veritable hail of bombs had glanced off the huge dome during the first half hour of the raid. From their vantage point, looking through a curtain of flames and dense smoke, it seemed as though the cathedral would soon be a blazing ruin along with its neighbours.

St Paul's was far from doomed, although it was still in great peril. The volunteers stayed out on the roof to take care of the steady flow of flying embers, while the regulars continued making the rounds with their usual thoroughness. Even though they were reinforced by the volunteers, the Cathedral Watch could not reach every fire bomb as soon as it fell. At 6.39, the control centre received a telephone call from Cannon Street Fire Station. The fire house switchboard reported that the dome was on fire.

At the cathedral, a team was sent out at once to investigate. They discovered that an incendiary had lodged itself in the outer dome. It had punched halfway through the lead covering with its tail fins still jutting through the outside, where it remained, sputtering and smoking profusely. The bomb was going to be a bit awkward to get at — it was halfway up the dome, and would be difficult to reach with a sandbag — but it was no serious threat. Even if the IB burned its way through and fell inside, it would come to rest on the paved aisle inside, where it could easily be smothered.

From outside the cathedral, however, it looked as though a major fire was burning fiercely within the giant hemisphere. The brilliant light of the smouldering bomb was reflected by the dome's outer shell, and the smoke, propelled by the strong breeze, added to the illusion. It seemed as if flames were being whipped into a blazing frenzy by gusts of wind, and that St Paul's had become a mass of fire.

One reporter was already at work writing the obituary. 'Tonight, the bomber planes of the German Third Reich hit London where it hurts the most — in the heart.' In a nearby City street, broadcast correspondent Edward R. Murrow of the Columbia Broadcasting System, New York, was preparing his nightly report to America. 'And the church that meant most to Londoners is gone. St Paul's Cathedral, built by Sir Christopher Wren, her great dome towering over the capital of the Empire, is burning to the ground as I talk to you now.'

Up in the dome, the fire watchers slowly worked their way toward the bomb. It had stopped sputtering by now, and was burning hot and steadily, melting the lead skin that held it in place. Before anyone could get close to it, the bomb fell outward, sliding down the great curving surface and landing in the Stone Gallery, the passageway that circles the bottom of the dome. There, it was easily disposed of by members of the Cathedral Watch. The intense heat given off by the incendiary had finally dislodged it, allowing it to fall out by its own weight, like a hot

"The sky was incandescent with red and orange ..." The towers of the Houses of Parliament and a lone barrage balloon are silhouetted against the fires.

knife in a block of butter. Some would later claim that this was a miracle. It was, in fact, only gravity.

The fire squad over at Guildhall also had its hands full. The light brown stone of the historic Great Hall looked the colour of red brick, reflecting the fires that were closing in steadily. Every member of the volunteer fire squad worked hard to keep the hall out of danger and, so far, had succeeded. Only one minor emergency occurred since the attack began, when the electricity failed at 6.45. The emergency generators were switched on at once, and power was quickly restored.

St Bride's Church, on Fleet Street, which had no fire squad, was not as fortunate. The church had been struck by incendiaries early in the raid, and its roof, along with the lower tiers of its graceful 'wedding cake' steeple, was now burning furiously.

The night porters at the adjacent Press Association, the Press Club, and Reuters News Service, ran inside St Bride's to rescue as much of the church's property as they could carry. The men made several trips inside and emerged each time with armloads of objects, including a brass lectern that had survived the Great Fire of 1666. No sooner had the last trip been made than the roof collapsed in a heap of fiery rubble. The bells of St Bride's, which only ninety minutes before had chimed out a hymn for the New Year, would soon afterwards plummet from their lofty steeple and smash to pieces on the floor.

The veteran pre-war Luftwaffe bomb-aimers and pilots, such as Hauptmann Friedrich Aschenbrenner and Major Schulz-Hein, were never content unless they were certain that every bomb dropped scored a bull's-eye, directly on-target. This attitude was not shared, however, by the young wartime conscripts. Most of these young men lacked the confidence, and also the combat experience, of their superiors. Their only concern was to get rid of their bombs and get the hell home before the flak or fighters got them.

Tonight's heavy anti-aircraft fire may not have been scoring any direct hits on the Luftwaffe's intruders, but it was doing a thorough job on the nerves of the green and untried Fliegern and Leutnants aboard the Ju88s and He111s. The flak was always an unnerving, but at the same time fascinating, sight. Tonight's cloud cover made it all the more frightening. Punching dramatically through the layer of overcast, the red-orange balls darted directly at the incoming aircraft, moving faster and faster as they approached. Then with a blinding yellow flash, the flak shells burst — thousands of feet below the bombers but close enough to rattle the inexperienced.

After flying above such a pyrotechnics display for about twenty minutes, since crossing the English coast, the state of mind of these young men was anything but settled. They were all too busy watching the shell fire, it seemed, to attend business. Conscripted bomb-aimers, hypnotised by the colourful and deadly display, adjusted bomb sights clumsily or not at all, incurring a tongue-lashing from an exasperated pilot. Pilots just out of training school misunderstood the instructions of their bomb-aimers and soared right past their aiming point.

Clusters of incendiaries fell as far south as Croydon, Surrey, twelve miles south of the City of London, and on Mrs Gwladys Cox's block of flats in Hampstead, five miles to the north. Many of these fire bombs burnt themselves out on the pavement or were put out by homeowners, but some struck locked-up shops and did considerable damage.

Such grossly inaccurate bombing was the exception, however, rather than the rule. Most of Luftflotte 3's aircrews were putting their bomb loads on or very near the target. Their attack was still gathering momentum, striking areas in the City and Southwark that had been untouched until now, and dropping still more of the two-pound incendiaries on districts already vividly aflame.

Transportation in the vicinity of the still spreading fire zone was almost at a standstill, but there were a few vehicles running. Special Constable R.E. Crowfoot was on his way into the City from his brother's house in Stoke Newington, heading directly into the fires. It was not the flames that troubled Crowfoot, however, but the smoke. When his trolley bus reached City Road, he checked the shield of his gas mask to make sure that it was intact.

"Whenever the wind shifted, the giant hemisphere changed color, from orange, to yellow, to red . . ." St. Paul's Cathedral from a Fleet Street rooftop, its dome illuminated by wind-blown flames. This photo, one of the most famous of the war, became a symbol of London's defiance in the Blitz.

Sixteen year-old Ron Woolaway had boarded the Number 35 tramcar at Camberwell Gate shortly after 6 p.m., beginning his daily shuttle. Every evening, he made the trip from his home to the public air raid shelter underneath the Strand, where he spent the night with his family. He had heard the air raid sirens, but everything seemed normal until he reached Blackfriars Road. From there, he could see a white glow to the north, created by hundreds of glittering incendiaries.

When the tram reached the middle of Westminster Bridge, the driver refused to go any further, insisting that it was too dangerous. He changed his mind after a few minutes, though, and the tram continued its interrupted route over Westminster Bridge and up the Victoria Embankment.

When it reached the corner of Horse Guards Avenue, its journey ended forever. A high-explosive bomb, 550 lbs of TNT, hit and exploded just behind the tram. The carriage was demolished. The driver, conductor, and all but three of its thirty-three passengers were killed instantly.

Ron Woolaway somehow survived the blast. He does not remember the explosion at all — the next thing he recalls is sitting on the running board of a taxi with his suit blown to shreds. Woolaway suffered chest injuries from the blast, and both of his eardrums had been broken. He was driven back across the river to St Thomas' Hospital, where he vaguely remembers being taken downstairs to the ward.

A short time after the fire crew at St Paul's safely disposed of the dome bomb, firemen from in and around the City began arriving in the fire zone to combat the infernos — the Fire Brigade had finally been called into action. At most stations the men had been aware of the fire situation, but could do nothing without orders. It would have been foolish for the fire appliances to fan out on their own, dispersing throughout a wide area and not being available when needed. In the boroughs surrounding the stricken area, firemen had been waiting for nearly forty-five minutes, tense and apprehensive, for their call. When it came, the men hurried to their appliances and were driven at breakneck speed toward the bright, steady light just beyond.

At Home Office Fire Control Room in Whitehall, the mobilising

'Some of the buildings along the Churchyard were only a matter of yards away.' Buildings along St Paul's Churchyard alight, with the Cathedral on the right. This shows how close the flames came to the Cathedral's walls.

'Firemen frantically manhandled gear . . .' The Auxiliary Fire Service at work, in a photo not taken on 29th December. The trailer pump, shown in picture, was the most widely used of all fire appliances.

staff of Fire Service Chief Sir Aylmer Firebrace was kept well advised of developments. London was being hit by a full-scale attack, not just another hit-and-run raid — in the City district a dangerous fire emergency was brewing up. It did not take long to appraise the reports coming in from the fire zone itself; even a single fire within the City boundary was cause for alarm. Every fire station within the hundred square mile London County Council region was put on alert. No fireman would be allowed to leave his station without express orders; in most cases, the orders were not long in coming.

Auxiliary Fireman James Mayes and his unit were among the first turned out. They left their station, Ambler Road School Station in Finsbury, just north of the City, and began racing toward the City boundary. Mayes and the rest of the pump's crew had no idea where their driver was taking them; usually, no officer bothered to tell a fireman, especially an auxiliary fireman, any more than absolutely necessary. Eventually they reached Guildhall, where all of Ambler Road School Station's vehicles came to a stop. Nothing was happening, so everybody got out and had a smoke.

While they were standing about, a Fire Brigade officer arrived, said they were not needed there, and split up the station's fire engines. Mayes' pump and one other were dispatched to Aldersgate Street Fire Station. When they arrived, the men found the station blazing hotly. As their first assignment, the crew set to work putting out a fire in a fire house.

Station Officer Laurence J. Odling of Whitefriars Fire Station, based at King's College on the Strand, did not wait for the bells to go down. He was well acquainted with the damage that an unattended fire bomb could cause, and sent his appliances out without waiting for orders. Station Officer Odling and his fire engines sped up the Strand toward Fleet Street, looking for a fire.

They did not have far to look. Almost as soon as they turned out the front gate, the ominous glow of a burning incendiary was seen coming from St Clement Danes church. The church, situated on an island in the middle of the Strand, had been badly damaged in an October Blitz raid. What was left of it was once again in

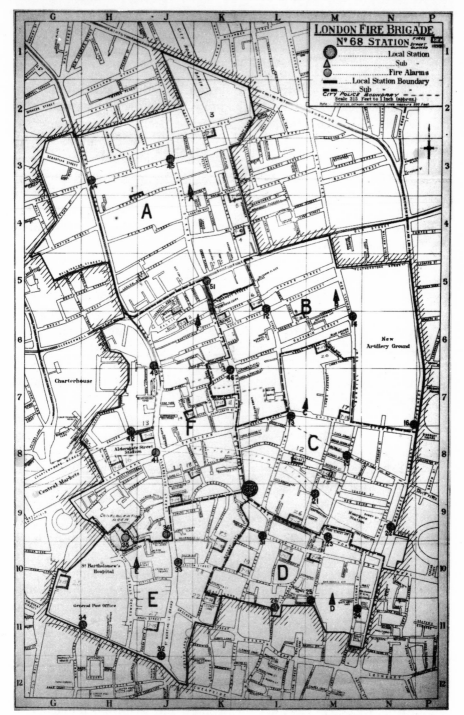

The incident map of Redcross Street Fire Station, LFB Station No. 68, for the night of 29th December, 1940. Paternoster Square and St Paul's Cathedral lie just south of Redcross Street Station's boundary, and Guildhall is by the southeastern corner, near fire alarm No. 26. The numbered circles indicate fire alarms, and triangles point out sub fire stations.

The squares marked 7—14 give the time and location of each fire bomb incident — 7—14 means a bomb struck at 7.14p.m. The first four incidents are logged at 7.09. Between 7.09 and 7.15, a total of six minutes, twenty-eight incidents had already come through Redcross Street Station's switchboard — an average of one every 13 seconds. This gives some idea of the volume of calls that swamped fire station telephones in the City and nearby districts.

danger. Odling's men went up on the roof and put out the smouldering bomb before it had the chance to work any damage.

On a night like this, everyone was expected to turn in his best effort; sometimes, a person was asked to give a little more than his best. Sub-Officer Frank Lawrence was spending a routine evening at Fire Brigade Headquarters, on the Albert Embankment in Lambeth. Unexpectedly, a senior officer approached and handed him a unique assignment. Lawrence was order to take two telephone operators, go up to Guildhall, and take over the City's Fire Control Centre.

Lawrence was taken aback at being given such a responsible job. He had been promoted to sub-officer only a few weeks before; until then, he had been an ordinary fireman, stationed at Redcross Street Station. The explanation he was given, that his two years at Redcross Street made him an expert on the City's tangle of alleyways and sidestreets, did little to ease his mind. But an order was an order, and Sub-Officer Lawrence was soon on his way across Lambeth Bridge, heading toward the deftly spreading flames.

When his car passed Horse Guards Avenue in its journey through Westminster along the Albert Embankment, Lawrence caught sight of Ron Woolaway's tram. He did not find out until afterward that his neighbour's son had been on board, and had been killed in the blast.

Although the anti-aircraft batteries were doing nothing more than upsetting a few of the Luftwaffe's inexperienced aircrews, the guns were having better luck than the RAF's night fighters. The two-man crews of 219 Squadron's dark, twin-engined Bristol Beaufighters had not spotted even one of the enemy intruders so far. From their cockpits, the pilots of the Beaufighters saw nothing except the same view that greeted the eyes of Luftflotte 3: endless cloud and bursting anti-aircraft shells and, in the distance, a sinister red glow that shone through the overcast.

Night-fighter Squadron 219's Beaufighters deliberately patrolled their wedge-shaped sector, which extended from south London to the Channel coast, keeping a sharp and well-trained eye peeled for any sign of aircraft. But this was a very large piece of ter-

(*Left*) Marjorie Thyer, Nursing Sister at University College Hospital, who walked from New Cross Gate to the City at the height of the raid. (*Right*) Ron Woolaway, one of the three survivors of the bombed tram on the Victoria Embankment.

'Paternoster Square was now a giant pyre,' as seen from the dome of St Paul's Cathedral.

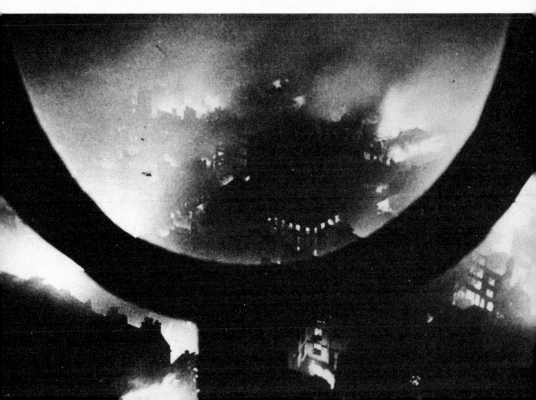

ritory for a mere squadron to protect. And on a black winter's night, an enemy bomber could be directly underneath or over-head, only 1,000 feet away, and still go unnoticed.

The Beaufighters were always in radio contact with Ground Controlled Interception (GCI) stations. These GCI stations, equipped with small radar sets of limited range, would vector a night fighter toward an unsuspecting intruder on its radar screen, putting the Beaufighter within immediate distance of the enemy aircraft. Night fighters were easily distinguishable from Luft-waffe bombers, since the fighters were fitted with IFF — Identi-fication of Friend from Foe — transmitters. The IFF made a splash on the radar which was visibly different from the blip of a Junkers or Heinkel. When the GCI controller made a hostile contact, he fed the course, speed, and height of the enemy bomber to a Beaufighter that was nearby, along with a course for inter-ception.

Tonight, 219 Squadron's fighters had been given several such interception courses. When a contact was received, the pilot pointed the nose of his fighter along the Ground Controller's vector, and the observer maintained a steady watch on the AI airborne radar. But when the Beaufighter came within what was supposed to have been radar range of the bogey — nothing. Nothing on the radar screen, nothing in sight. It was becoming a highly frustrating procedure.

Despite their lack of success, the night fighters kept in constant touch with the GCI stations, routinely investigating the Ground Controller's contacts. The pilots would keep trying until their fuel gauges let them know that it was time to return to Tangmere airfield. With any luck, one of the GCI vectors might point the way toward a solid, visible target.

The first units of the London Fire Brigade were now in position. Firemen frantically manhandled gear and linked their pumps to fire hydrants, turning thin streams of water on buildings that flamed high above their heads. But the firemen were not alone in their frenzy of activity. Throughout the fire zone, civilians also had all they could cope with. On Old Street, Stanley G. Champion was having a lively time. His sprint from his firm, Jackson Brothers, to the Auxiliary Fire Station in Baltic Street was quickened by clusters of incendiaries that kept popping all around him. It did not take him long to reach the AFS post, where he unceremoniously reported the fire, and then turned back toward his building.

On his way back, Champion had a chance to pause and take a look round. He could see dozens of buildings in flames along Old Street and on adjoining streets. The swish and clatter of falling incendiaries were almost continuous, and the sky was coloured an angry, unreal red. The white sparkling bombs on the roadway and pavement added to the glare. Champion thought there must have been thousands of them.

Across the river in Southwark, Frank Paling had a personal reason to be alarmed. His wife's mother lived in the City, in a six-storey block of flats in Aldersgate Street; from his place, he could see that the area was solidly aflame. Mr Paling decided to go up and make sure that everything was all right, setting out on foot across Blackfriars Bridge.

Not that the situation in Southwark was any better than in the City. The entire district from Waterloo Station eastward beyond London Bridge was laced with flame. Large squat warehouses flared dramatically, hurling great red and yellow pillars of flame into the night, and pouring out clouds of thick grey smoke. Mrs Rose Rich was still stranded in the local shelter near London Bridge, unable to get across the Thames to the Monument Underground Station. Mrs Rich had been in the shelter about half an hour, and people were talking about how ugly the scene outside looked, when she and the other occupants were ordered out. The shelter was not safe enough, everyone was told. They were ordered to run across to the deep shelter. With a minimum of fuss, the shelterers got up and silently but anxiously moved into the street.

It was every bit as bad as everyone had been told. The air outside was hot and acrid, and Mrs Rich could see great fires raging on both sides of the river. She was very frightened but, after bracing herself, 'ran like hell and made it' across to the deep shelter. Here, Mrs Rich would be safe for the time being, at least.

By this time, all railway traffic had stopped completely. Marjorie Thyer's train trip from Brighton to University College Hospital had become completely bogged down. She had reached East Croydon, Surrey, without very much trouble, travelling at a snail's pace in a crowded and almost pitch dark train. At East Croydon, she managed to get a train bound for Charing Cross Station, in London. But Nurse Thyer's train only got as far as New Cross, near Greenwich and about five miles from Charing Cross, when everyone was turned out with the announcement, 'All out! All out! Bomb on the line!' From there on, it was everyone for themselves.

Some people seemed to have all the luck. While Marjorie Thyer was enduring her slow and bumpy train ride, Mrs Eileen McConville had no trouble at all getting from Waterloo Station to Ewell, Surrey. Hers must have been the last train out of the station. It departed right on time and encountered no problems along its route.

And there were still a few, living inside the City of London's boundary, who could not figure out what all the fuss was about. Patricia Hutchings lived at Grocers Hall, just off Princes Street near the Bank of England, a Company Hall that now served as an Air Raid Warden Post as well. For the past forty-five minutes, the building's wardens and fire watchers had been collecting all the sandbags they could find and carrying them up to the roof. Patricia Hutchings was curious about all the activity, so she put her tin hat on and went up for a look. From the roof of Grocers Hall she could see men standing on many of the flat-roofed buildings in the area — the flames within the City made it seem more like late afternoon than night. All of them were busily dropping sand bags on bursting fire bombs.

Most of the people in the fire zone, however, were beyond the point of idle curiosity, especially the firemen, whose night was only just beginning. Station Officer Laurence J. Odling and the firemen from Whitefriars Fire Station, after putting out an incendiary that hit St Clement Danes Church, continued to work their way along Fleet Street, putting out fires as they came to them.

The other crews and appliances that left the station with Station Officer Odling had since dispersed throughout the area, with each unit tackling separate outbreaks of fire. Odling and his crew of four also were now operating independently, and had put out about half dozen combustions so far. Each one had taken a little longer to deal with than the last, as the flames spread and began to take hold.

# CHAPTER SIX

# 'That Won't Be There in the Morning'
## *7pm – 7.30pm*

By 7 p.m. Feldmarschall Hugo Sperrle had accomplished one of his main purposes in attacking the City. The General Post Office on King Edward Street, with its telephone and telegraph cables and all of its communications links, was being abandoned; all postal employees were sent home. It had taken roughly one hour for the bombers of Sperrle's Air Luftflotte 3 to sever London's most important tie with the rest of Britain and overseas. Postman L.E. Benning was among those given an 'early night away' because of the air raid. Benning and a co-worker left the post office and went to get a trolley bus to East Ham; along the way, the two imagined that the fire bombs were chasing after them.

As things stood, three separate conflagrations raged: an area stretching from Fleet Street to Moorgate and north into the Barbican, nearly three-quarters of a mile long and a quarter-mile wide; another area over by the Tower, centred around the Minories; and a mile-long swath of fire in Southwark, between Waterloo Station and Tower Bridge. Also, isloated outbreaks blazed away in scattered spots outside and in between these three infernos. A strong wind from the south-west continued to fan the flames. And the bombers of Luftflotte 3 kept on passing overhead, dropping fresh clusters of incendiaries, starting more outbreaks of fire.

The lit-up switchboard at Guildhall's control centre told the story at a glance. All the lines were already jammed by the time Sub-Officer Frank Lawrence and his telephonists arrived from Headquarters, Lambeth. Between 6.27 and 7.00 more than eighty calls reported outbreaks of fire, mostly from the City's EC2 district.

Elsewhere, senior officers of London's fire staff were feverishly attempting to organise an attack against the blitz. Divisional

Officer Francis Peel, in charge of the LFB's Northern Division administration, began phoning up each of the district stations under his charge to ask about the fire situation. Divisional Officer Peel arranged his own makeshift, but effective, method of plotting the intensity of the wartime fires. As each station gave its report, a series of pins would be stuck into a large map of London — one pin for each address where a fire had been reported. In a short while, a visual image of the fireman's battleground would take shape, giving Peel and his staff the chance to size up the situation and plan their first move.

It did not take very long before a cluster of pins had accumulated around the City and its immediate vicinity on Francis Peel's map. Divisional Officer Peel and his assistant, Kenneth Newcombe Hoare, decided that a visit to the fire area should be made, in order to get a first-hand look at the fires. The way things were shaping up, it would probably be necessary to fight this conflagration as an area, literally a 'fire zone', rather than a series of individual addresses.

For the London Fire Brigade's regular firemen and auxiliaries, however, there was no time to wait for strategic directives. Guildhall's control room had received its own hundredth fire call at 7.10; the telephone operators calmly and methodically relayed the calls for Fire Brigade posts as quickly as possible. In the stations scattered throughout London, telephones sprang into life as soon as Guildhall's operators dispatched the fire bulletins. As soon as the calls came in the bells went down and the trailer pumps and turntable ladders began their race through the blacked-out streets, toward the red-orange flames in the distance.

Sub-Officer Richard B. Horne, attached to an emergency fire station in Wandsworth, south of the Thames, was ordered to report to Whitefriars Fire Station with two heavy units. He had no idea how bad tonight's raid was until he reached the bend in the river just east of Chelsea Bridge, where the mud of the river bank at low tide reflected the redness beyond. Several buildings along the way were burning steadily, but had to be passed by — Horne's orders were to proceed directly to Whitefriars.

When he reached the Fire Station, Horne found the Mobilising Officer and five firewomen absorbed in answering calls by the light of a few sweating candles. He asked the Mobilising Officer where to report. The officer pointed to the flags on the map and told Horne to take his pick.

'Is anything priority?' Horne asked.

'Practically all of it,' the officer replied. He then pointed to Gough Square, off Fleet Street, the site of several factories and also the home of Dr Samuel Johnson, the eighteenth-century compiler of the famous dictionary, and mentioned that it was quite important. He added that there was a dire water shortage. All that could be done until water relays from the Thames were set up would be to kick the fire bombs off the roof.

Horne did not have to wait until he reached Gough Square to start disposing of incendiaries. When he went outside to his two heavy fire pumps, his men were already kicking them off the machines. The bombs continued to blossom in fiery clusters all throughout the short trip to their destination, lighting up the roads 'like fairyland'.

The Mobilising Officer at Whitefriars was not overstating the case when he described the water shortage as 'dire'. The supply was dangerously low. A high explosive bomb, one of the few dropped so far, had cracked the City's primary water main somewhere along its two-mile length, between the Grand Union Canal in Islington and the River Thames near Cannon Street Railway Station. The twenty-four-inch pipe would be useless for quite some time.

An incredible drain was placed upon the water mains that were still intact because of the loss of the City main. So many fire appliances linked up to the existing mains that the water pressure failed. The large, cast iron pipe that ran under Upper Thames Street was among those that were tapped out. It had more than adequate pressure when the first fires broke out, but after more than one hundred fire engines took up positions along the main, the water taken by these pumps was more than the pipeline could ever supply — the pressure in the line dropped to zero. Even though it was not damaged, a well-aimed enemy bomb could not have done a neater job. With the City main fractured, and the existing mains tapped dry, the fire zone was cut off from its water resources.

But even the section of the City that still had water pressure, mostly in the western part of the district, still blazed out of control. Fireman James Goldsmith, at Redcross Street Fire Station, was given no specific orders; he and his fellows were told simply to do what they could, and pick their fire when they came to it. There were plenty of fires right in the vicinity of the station, so they went to work in nearby Jewin Street.

It soon became apparent that they were losing the battle on all fronts. The firemen could not gain access to the burning buildings. Doors were double padlocked, and bars blocked the windows. They did their best to fight the flames from out in the street, but to no avail. Fireman Goldsmith could see that he and his mates were not really extinguishing the fires at all — they were only pushing them eastward toward Redcross Street.

Everything, every street and every building, within a quarter mile radius of Redcross Street Station would soon afterward burn in one vast, vivid flame. Entire streets within this area — Milton Street; Coleman Street; Moor Lane; the Barbican; and a host of small alleyways — were already lined with furiously blazing shops, flats, and office blocks. Once in a while, a fire-weakened building would flare up suddenly in a brilliant burst of yellow and, immediately afterward, crash down into the street with a teeth clenching roar. Feldmarschall Sperrle's calculations had been close to perfect. His fire raid was succeeding better than he ever could have hoped, or the London Fire Brigade ever could have feared.

The area just to the south-west was faring just as badly. Paternoster Square was now a giant pyre. Carter Lane and the Old Change and almost all that surrounded St Paul's flamed out of control. Only St Paul's itself was not ablaze, standing in the centre of the inferno, but who could tell how long the great cathedral would remain unscathed.

If any onlookers were able to remember their schoolbook history at such a time, the sight of St Paul's lit up by fires all round was anything but an inspiration. In the Great Fire of 1666, Old St Paul's stood unharmed for several days while the same area that now burned again — Creed Lane, Ave Maria Lane, Amen Court — were lighted torches. But Old St Paul's did succumb to the irresistible flames on the third day of the Great Fire, just as Christopher

Wren's cathedral seemed on the brink of giving in to
the Luftwaffe's onslaught.

'Old Paul's' may have taken a long time to die, but when it
fell, it fell dramatically. Like the Wren cathedral, Old St Paul's
was covered by a roof made of lead-covered wood. The wooden
roof timbers were where the flames first took hold. Before long
the six acres of roofing beams burned from end to end. In the
intense heat, the layers of lead covering the timber started to melt,
running down the sides and into cracks in the cathedral walls.
When the molten metal poured into the cracks and fissures, the
sudden heat caused the masonry to expand violently. The walls
began exploding — great chunks of Caen stone, some weighing
100 pounds or more, soared through the air like cannon balls.
For an entire day the old church continued to burn, until nothing
stood except the fire-blackened bones of its skeleton.

It was an uncomfortable precedent. Even now, the walls of
St Paul's, and the lead roofs, were hot enough to cause concern.
And the temperature of the air kept increasing. On three sides of
the cathedral, buildings burned uncontrollably, blazing hot and
steadily. Some of the buildings along the churchyard were only a
matter of yards away.

Fireman W. Callaghan, from Manchester Square Fire Station in
the West End, had, like Sub-Officer Richard Horne from Wandsworth, been dispatched to Whitefriars Fire Station. From there,
he and his crew were immediately sent out on a fire call. On their
way outbound, they caught their first glimpse of St Paul's, brightly
lit up by flaming, disintegrating buildings. As they sped by,
Callaghan nodded toward the cathedral and told the fireman next
to him, 'That won't be there in the morning.'

Ironically, the roof patrols in the cathedral were not able to see
very much of the surrounding fires. The dense smoke blotted out
most of the view. It was just as well, since nobody had much time
for sightseeing tonight, although George Garwood watched the
Central Telephone Exchange on Wood Street burn down, 'without
a bucket of water to put on it.'

The crisis of the dome fire bomb had passed, but the cathedral
was still in danger. From the south, the blazing hulks sent a steady
stream of hot embers onto the roofs, which the patrols continued

to smother with wet sacks. Inside, the regulars of the Cathedral Watch still made their routine checks of the dome, hearing the distorted sounds of anti-aircraft fire and the droning of countless aircraft engines, all of which seemed magnified inside the huge hemisphere. It was all normal by now, even the guns and the bombs. The only thing different tonight was the eerie reddish light that penetrated everywhere.

One of the most famous onlookers to the Great Fire of 1666 was Samuel Pepys, who described the City's ordeal in his celebrated Diary. His account, written more than 270 years before, might well have been written by an eyewitness of the Luftwaffe's aerial assault:

> We [went] to a little alehouse on the Bankside, over against the Three Cranes, [on the Thames' south bank, opposite Three Cranes Wharf] and there stayed until it was dark almost, and saw the fire grow; and, as it grew darker, [the fire] appeared more and more: in corners and upon steeples, and between churches and houses, as far as we could see up the hill of the City. A most horrid and malicious bloody flame, not like the fine flame of an ordinary fire ... We stayed 'til, it being darkish, we saw the fire as only one entire arch of fire from this to the other side of the [London] Bridge, and in a bow up the hill in an arch above a mile long. It made me weep to see it.

The heavy volume of incoming calls allowed the Fire Brigade to send only one pump to each fire in most cases — usually pitifully insufficient. At Jackson Brothers, Ltd., up on Old Street, the AFS was finally able to answer Stanley G. Champion's call. A commandeered taxi towing a trailer pump came to an abrupt halt in front of the burning textile firm, and the crew of three set to work at once. But three men could do little to halt such a blaze, which would have drawn several heavy units in peace-time. Tonight, however, the heavy pumps were not available. Although the firemen did their best, Jackson Brothers continued to burn out of control.

Even though senior Fire Brigade officers tried vainly to organise some sort of co-ordinated operation, chaos reigned on the fire

ground. The fires were spreading and growing so swiftly that it
was difficult to keep up to date. A fire engine would be sent to an
address, but by the time the pump arrived that building, and
usually its neighbours, would be flaming from basement to roof.
The firemen, having no other orders, would stay at the address to
which they had been sent, even though, in many cases, there was
no water in the hydrants. In Whitecross Street, over a dozen units
were trapped when fire-eroded buildings collapsed into the street,
cutting off all lanes of exit. All the crews managed to crawl to
safety, but their appliances were lost. And there were few enough
fire appliances available to begin with.

A quarter mile south of Whitecross Street, Guildhall was still
holding its own, although the roof spotters could see burning
buildings to the east, west, and north. Sometime after 7 p.m.,
the Church of St Lawrence Jewry, just to the south in Guildhall
Yard, was struck by an incendiary bomb in its steeple. The brightly
flaring bomb was spotted at once by Guildhall's observers, along
with the fact that no one was on hand to take care of it. A report
was relayed at once to Cannon Street Fire Station. But no one
from Guildhall's crew was sent over to see about it. No one
could be spared. Besides, the empty church was securely locked
and bolted – no one would have been able to get inside, much less
climb up into the steeple to extinguish the bomb.

Apart from the visual spectacle, the inferno also produced a
range of sounds and dissonances. If the flames were awesome and,
to some, malignantly beautiful, the din they created was singularly
unpleasant, although not everyone heard their doom song in the
same way. Some heard the still growing flames as a loud, frightening, cracking-popping noise. To others the blaze roared and sighed,
like forced human breathing, or roared in a constant low tone.

Along with the guttural noises of the fire, there throbbed the
steady drum-drumming of the fire pumps, from the areas that
still had a water supply. Every once in a while, the whole caco-
phony was underscored by the crash of a fire-weakened wall. And
always there was the constant hollow drone of the bombers winging
their way over the target. One noise, however, had stopped: the
roaring bark of the anti-aircraft batteries halted abruptly, all of
them at once. The silence of the guns was strange to the ears that

had grown used to the muzzle blast, as though a dripping faucet or whistling radiator had been suddenly shut off.

The anti-aircraft network that was supposed to protect London, as well as all of Britain, was a total failure. Even General Sir Fredrick Pile, in charge of Anti-Aircraft Command, admitted that the system was 'no good'. The guns were averaging only one hit for every several thousand shells fired, and damage to roofing tiles and skylights was worse than anything inflicted upon the Luftwaffe.

Yet the flak was a great morale builder for Londoners. The nightly bang-bang-banging away at the raiders gave everyone the feeling that they were hitting back. And sometimes the flak batteries did pick off a raider during their nightly display.

But now, suddenly, the guns were silent. The raid was far from over, anyone could see that. Still, someone had obviously given the order to stop firing. Onlookers and shelterers in the vicinity of the anti-aircraft guns wondered why their guns had stopped shooting back at the enemy who was trying to burn down their city.

Someone had indeed ordered the guns to cease fire. The order came directly from Fighter Command at Stanmore, Middlesex. The Operations Staff had not given up the fight, however; in fact, just the opposite.

Along with the directive to Anti-Aircraft Command, the Operations Officer at Stanmore had also sent a message through to Gravesend, Kent, the airfield of Number 85 Fighter Squadron. Gravesend's squadron of Hawker Hurricanes were being sent directly over London to intercept the Luftwaffe. Joining 85 Squadron would be the Beaufighters of 219 Squadron, already up over Surrey, which were now called in to patrol over the capital.

Because of the fighters, London's anti-aircraft had to be called off. For although the guns were seldom lucky enough to hit an enemy bomber, there was still a chance, however slim, that they might unluckily shoot down one of the RAF's own aircraft.

As soon as they got their 'scramble', the young pilots of 85 Squadron climbed aboard their Hurricane fighters and coaxed their engines to life. One after another, the low-winged, single-engine aircraft roared down Gravesend's runway and into the murky Kentish sky. The Hurricanes had no radar at all; since there was no moon tonight, there was not much chance of anyone sighting anything in the dark. But each fighter mounted eight .303 machine guns, and the young men who flew them, though no experts yet, were fast learning the art of night combat.

It took only a few minutes for the Hurricanes to reach their station — Gravesend is only about 25 miles east of the City. The pilots needed no one to direct them toward their patrol area. London's fires were clearly visible during their 6,000 foot climb into the clouds.

The inferno was just as distinct after the Hurricanes had risen above the layers of overcast sky. The waves of hot air from the hundreds of fires welled right up through the layer, boring a hole in the middle of the fleecy grey and causing mild turbulence. Although 85 Squadron had flown many combat missions during the Battle of Britain, none of the men had seen anything like this before. The glare from the fires below, and the heat and smoke that churned through the clouds and buffeted their fighters when they flew over it, angered some of the men and made others cold with fear. The veterans could recall the summer just past, when their own airfield had been attacked. During the bright, cloudless days, the bombers with the black crosses came and dropped their bombs, and buildings burned and men died, the same as tonight.

People in outlying districts throughout Greater London were also becoming aware of the strange redness in the sky. Residents of Chiswick and Walthamstow and Battersea could see that this was not their raid. The redness in the sky was nothing more than an object of curiosity. The Luftwaffe kept on with its stream of bombers, but caused no great alarm. Tonight, the fires were someone else's worry.

Roof spotters near the fire ground did not have the luxury of being objective. Brilliant, steady flames soared higher than their rooftops, and seemed to grow higher and brighter as they looked on. The canopy of smoke that hung over the area made the flames even more radiant, reflecting the glare like a light shone in a fog, bathing everything in a lurid blood red. Bits of glowing embers blew through the air, sharp, vivid darts contrasting with the fierce afterglow.

Lodgers in air raid shelters in and around the fire zone could not see the relentless flames, but word of the intensive bombing filtered down to them. It was usual for some of the 'braver persons' to go up and have a look whenever there was an air raid. When Eileen Waterman's father heard the news in Banner Street's community shelter, he went back to his flat to rescue his insurance policies. In a basement shelter on Farringdon Road, Miss M. Ferriter heard that the 'whole City is on fire'. But she was not impressed. She had heard the same report many times during the past few months.

Directly across the River Thames from the City, the Borough of Southwark was undergoing an almost identical ordeal. The river bank's line of old warehouses and other buildings now burned viciously. Near Guy's Hospital, Edith Stannet and her husband joined a bucket brigade and put out a small fire near their coffee shop. Across from London Bridge Station, a warehouse had been hit by incendiaries and was vividly aflame. The shelterers from the station also formed a bucket brigade, pouring pails of water on the flames until the Fire Brigade arrived. They were not putting out the fire, but at least it was better than sitting and listening to the bombing from inside the shelter.

The interior levels of London Bridge Station were becoming more and more uncomfortable. The already stagnant air was becoming hot, and the heat, along with rumours of terrible bomb damage, confused and frightened the crowd of shelterers. At about the same time that the bucket brigade volunteers were keeping themselves busy, the warden in charge of the shelter made an announcement: anyone wishing to take the chance would be allowed to cross over London Bridge to the Monument Underground Station, on the north side of the Thames. Mrs Rose Rich, who had been trying to reach the Monument Station since 6 p.m., decided to make the trip, along with one other person, a man who kept repeating that he had to get to St Mary's Underground Station. St Mary's Station, between Whitechapel and Aldgate East, had been closed since before the war, but Mrs Rich did not ask why he wanted to go there. She was glad to have a companion.

The two of them walked outside into the hot, stifling air. Mrs Rich's friend grabbed her hand and, when the wind blew the fire back, they began their dash across the bridge. They were only about halfway across when the wind shifted again, engulfing London Bridge in a swirl of flames, sending both of them running back while firemen sprayed them with jets of water. Both Mrs Rich and her companion were soaking wet and out of breath when they got back, and had singed hair from their adventure. It would be quite a while before they would be allowed to try again.

Outside New Cross Station in south-eastern London, Nurse Marjorie Thyer was having a similar problem. Her train, originally bound for Charing Cross Station, had dumped her off several miles from her destination, which was University College Hospital. Now, she did not know which way to turn. Except for the muzzle flashes of the steadily pounding anti-aircraft guns, all the roadways had been inky black. The only bus she had seen was a local. When she hopefully asked the driver if there were any buses into Central London, she was told, 'Not a hope. Nothing can get through', but Nurse Thyer was determined to reach the hospital, so she began walking toward the russet glow in the western sky.

Several miles to the west, Frank Paling was crossing Blackfriars Bridge all alone, walking into the City to look for his wife's mother. By the time he reached the block of flats where she lived, in Aldersgate Street, the building was a fiery ruin. It looked as though every one of the burnt out six floors had caved into the basement. Paling had no idea where his mother in law had gone or what had happened to her. He was not even sure if she was still alive. Hoping for the best, he set out for nearby Snow Hill Police Station to begin making inquiries.

Oberleutnant Dieter Heibing of Kampfgeschwader 51, had already dropped his bomb load and was heading back toward France. Although his mission had been completed, Oberleutnant Heibing knew all too well that his night would not be over until he set his Ju88 safely down on the runway at Etampes, south of Paris.

The sudden let-up in the anti-aircraft fire, which had happened before the bomb-aimer began the run-in, made Heibing suspicious. He had never seen the flak drop off all at once like that before —

something must be up. Heibing ordered his two man aircrew to keep awake, and to report anything unusual at once.

Soon after the Junkers turned onto its homeward course, the radio operator, facing rearward in the dorsal gunner's seat, sighted two lights, close together and vaguely ominous, off to the left. He did not know what the twin dashes were, but he knew that they did not belong there. The two spots certainly were not stars — they seemed to be closing in on him. After a short while, it became obvious that the lights were the exhausts of a twin-engined aircraft. But why was it behaving so oddly? Maybe it was a Junkers in trouble. It did not look like a Heinkel or, for that matter, did not look much like a Junkers, either. After a last, long look, it finally dawned on him what the oncoming aircraft was.

'*Achtung! Jäger! Zur linken!*' exploded in the headsets of the pilot and navigator. Heads and eyes turned quickly, and muscles involuntarily tensed. Oberleutnant Heibing snapped a glance over his left shoulder and, right where the radioman said it would be, on the Junkers' port quarter, saw the dark, snub-nosed silhouette of a Bristol Beaufighter. The twin-engined fighter was several hundred yards away and closing fast.

Oberleutnant Heibing pushed the control column sharply forward and snapped the rudder full left, throwing the Junkers into a diving, tight left turn. His best chance was to dip directly underneath the attacking fighter and keep diving, all the way underneath the cloud cover if necessary. The Englishman was too close to attempt outrunning him. As the Junkers banked and dove sharply, Heibing saw the Beaufighter erupt with violent splashes of flame; a second later, a stream of cannon shells and tracer bullets darted harmlessly overhead.

The Junkers kept plunging for several thousand feet, almost to the tops of the clouds. Only when he was thoroughly convinced that he had lost the Beaufighter, and his wireless operator reported that he could see no sign of aircraft, did Oberleutnant Heibing resume his interrupted journey to Étampes. Everyone had been slightly shaken by the encounter but, aside from that, was none the worse off. They would all get a chance to catch their breath during the trip back to base. The hot food and coffee in the officers' mess would certainly go down well after this fracas.

No one who was unlucky enough to be within Feldmarschall Sperrle's target zone was being given the chance to catch their breath. New clusters of fire bombs kept on landing with their gaudy white sparklers, keeping the few roof watchers that were on duty this Sunday night very busy. A sharp-eyed fire spotter could sight an incendiary bomb as soon as it struck, saving considerable property, and sometimes lives, from flames. From their rooftop station in Dowgate Dock, by Cannon Street Station, Benjamin Davis and his partner saw an incendiary penetrate the roof of an adjacent building, the old Three Cranes Wharf.

In the Middle Ages there really were three cranes, three loading derricks, on the wharf, for hoisting goods aboard Thames freight barges. Before the 1666 fire, a well known tavern called the Three Cranes Vintry stood near the wharf; the inn vanished in the Great Fire. Now, the Three Cranes was once again in peril, from a fire of a more sinister nature.

As soon as he saw the fire bomb hit, Ben Davis hurried down into the street, ran up Dowgate Hill while hugging a wall for protection, and found a policeman huddled in a doorway at the top of the hill. He was not hard to find — Davis thinks this policeman must have been the fattest man on the City force. Davis reported the bomb, but the policeman apparently was not convinced and wanted to see for himself. So Mr Davis quickly agreed to show him, and led the policeman down Dowgate Hill.

The overweight constable had no trouble going down the hill, but climbing the eight flights of stairs to Ben Davis' roof post was a different matter. He slowly gasped along, stopping to get his wind every few minutes and swearing a blue streak all the way, but eventually he pulled himself up onto the roof. He was shown the smoke filtering out of Three Cranes Wharf and, satisfied, went to get the 'heavy gang' — a special squad equipped to break through heavy padlocks — climbing down from the roof with a good deal less trouble than he had coming up.

The fire crew at Guildhall, only a few blocks north of Dowgate Hill, had done an equally praiseworthy job of saving their own building from any serious damage. The hall, situated in the heart of the still-expanding fire zone, was surrounded by collapsing, flame-ruined buildings, but was still untouched by flames itself.

The volunteer fire watchers could see that their night was far from over, however. Fireguard R.C.M. Fitzhugh gives this impression of the attack from Guildhall's roof:

> The block bounded by Bassishaw House, Fore Street, Alder-manbury, and Basinghall Street appeared to be one solid mass of flame. St Stephen's, Coleman Street, was soon enveloped in flames, and we could see the steeple and weather cock fall. Fires were everywhere in the City area. From time to time, heavy high explosive bombs or land mines were dropped ... There would be the sound of something rushing through the air — then a brilliant flash would light up the entire sky and horizon and followed within two or three seconds by the most resounding explosion.

Nobody was doing anything about the fire bomb lodged in the steeple of St Lawrence Jewry, in Guildhall Yard. The Fire Brigade had still not arrived, and the Guildhall Squad had its own duties. The bomb was reported to have almost burned itself out by 7.15, although small flames could be seen from time to time. By 7.30, Commander F.A. George of Guildhall's Fire Squad noted that the church steeple was 'well alight', and that the Fire Brigade had still not arrived.

# CHAPTER SEVEN

# 'We'll Be Back Later'
## *7.30pm – 8.30pm*

Cannon Street Fire Station's failure to respond to Guildhall's alarms had nothing to do with laxness or inefficiency. The fact was that the firehouse had no one on hand to send to St Lawrence Jewry's church to investigate Guildhall's report. The Fire Brigade was fighting two battles at the same time. The first battle was against the flames, which was more than enough by itself. The second, equally serious, was against shortages — shortages of manpower and equipment, and of water. By 7.30, only an hour and twenty minutes after the 'fire raisers' of KG100 dropped their bombs, it was clear that both battles were being lost.

Water pressure was the most critical problem. That lucky hit on the City's primary water main had disrupted the entire district; pressure in the still-intact lines remained at zero. There were stagnant water mains dotted about, but these were not large enough or numerous enough to even begin solving the issue. The most logical source of water under the circumstances was the River Thames. But the river was at an abnormally low tide tonight, and it would not be easy to set up relays for the pumps. There was not much choice, however — it was either a little water from the Thames or no water at all — so teams were set up to pump water from the river at several points between Blackfriars and Tower Bridge. Assistant Divisional Officer Geoffrey Blackstone, a tall, muscular, old line 'smoke-eating' fireman, was supervising a relay operation near London Bridge, trying desperately to pump enough water towards the uncontrolled fires that threatened Guy's Hospital in Southwark.

One of the many problems with trying to pump Thames River water was that it took too much time. Lengths of hose pipe had to be dragged through many yards of thick, slippery mud before the unnaturally low river was reached. Firemen slipped and stumbled under their loads, inching along at an agonising pace. All the while, flames on both sides of the Thames were taking a better hold and spreading.

Feldmarschall Hugo Sperrle's strategy — dropping masses of fire bombs on the week-end before New Year when tides were at their lowest point — was working splendidly. Luftflotte 3's Heinkels and Junkers may have set the fires, but the absence of water and London's weekday inhabitants had done the rest. Also, luck had a hand in the game. If that one 550 lb bomb had not cracked the City's 24-inch main, the supply of water into the fire ground might have been substantial enough to make a difference.

In his suite at the Hotel Luxembourg in Paris, Feldmarschall Sperrle was not fully aware of the damage done by his bombers. He had heard reports from the bomber crews that the target was fiercely alight but, because of the cloud cover, these visual reports were imprecise. Even so, Sperrle and his staff had no reason to worry. The second wave of bombers, which would blast the target apart with a storm of high-explosive bombs, would finish off anything left standing by the fires.

The London Fire Brigade had enough to worry about already. All of the City's five fire stations were swamped with calls, so many that the firewomen at the switchboards had to make each one wait its turn. And when the call finally did come through, there was nothing that the firewomen could do except write down the address of the reported fire; every fire engine in every station within the 'square mile' had gone out long before, and there was nothing else to send, not even a single trailer pump.

In Guildhall Yard, the fire in St Lawrence Jewry's steeple still burned steadily and unattended. Guildhall itself still stood ominously untouched, but its crew of fire watchers kept a watchful eye on the flames which threatened from only a few yards away. At 7.40, ten minutes after Commander F.A. George noticed that the church was alight, the control room sent out a call to Redcross Street Fire Station. The results were the same as when Cannon Street Station had been called: all appliances had been sent out and, regrettably, there would be none available until reserves arrived from other parts of London.

Guildhall's telephone operators would have received the same reply no matter what station they contacted in the City or southern Islington. After the alarm had been received and the bells went down, all fire appliances had been dispatched to destinations within the fire zone. Only the station staff — mostly firewomen to answer the switchboard, along with the mobilising officer and one or two others — remained on hand. Ironically, three of the City's five fire stations were themselves threatened by flames, with no one to deal with them. Redcross Street Station was squarely in the middle of the fire-swept wilderness, and had more than its own share of troubles. The air inside was becoming uncomfortably warm; the lights and telephone lines were expected to go at any time. At one point, the station roof even caught fire.

The firemen were not the only ones with problems. Frank Paling had made the journey from his home in Southwark to Aldersgate Street, looking for his wife's mother. He found his mother-in-law's block of flats reduced to an abandoned, burnt-out shell. Not sure of where to look next, Paling had gone directly to Snow Hill Police Station to inquire about the missing party. The police weren't able to tell him anything, and sent him off to a nearby ARP headquarters. The Air Raid Wardens were a bit more helpful. They had a list of people who had been in the same shelter as Paling's mother-in-law, but could only advise him that these people had been taken to Clerkenwell, about a half-mile to the north.

Paling had been walking through the fire ground, jumping over hose pipes and around piles of masonry and rubble, for nearly an hour. He was tired and, although he had not been injured, he did not want to press his luck by walking through to Clerkenwell. Everything would be more settled in the morning, he reasoned, when there would also be more time to make a thorough search. With these thoughts in mind, Frank Paling decided to go back home to Southwark until then and get some sleep.

Southwark was enduring an avalanche of fire bombs almost as intense as the City's; everything that missed the 'square mile' landed on its neighbour across the river. The section where Frank Paling lived, near Blackfriars Bridge, had been pelted with a minor torrent of incendiaries, but was not nearly as bad as the district just to the east, between Southwark and London Bridges. Station Officer Thomas Bell, in charge of Southwark Fire Station, had his hands full with scores of combustions that had broken out everywhere at once. The fires in the grain and hops warehouses on Borough High Street were particularly troublesome and persistent. Not only did grain fires burn with a very hot flame, but the burnt wheat produced a gum-like residue that was so sticky that it clung to a fireman's boots, making for tricky walking. Station Officer Bell was so pre-occupied with his own worries that he did not realise that the City was catching most of the fury.

Just off Borough High Street, Guy's Hospital had several outbreaks of fire. The roof of the nurses' quarters was set alight in three places; this outbreak was tackled by all available staff members. Some other small fires also sprang up, but were put out before they got out of hand. Suffocating heat and day-like brightness from flames all round made the patients in the wards aware of the danger; plans were drawn up for the possible evacuation of the hospital.

The London Fire Brigade, with Geoffrey Blackstone in charge, was on the scene, but were handicapped by dry fire hydrants. Blackstone's men still struggled through the mud of the river bank to set up a water relay from the Thames to the endangered hospital. After a long, exhausting time, the link was established. Water was finally available, in fits and starts, to the Guy's Hospital — Borough High Street area. Whether or not it had come in time to save the hospital, however, was still the question.

Thousands of feet above the smoking ruins, the twin-engined bombers of Hugo Sperrle's Luftflotte 3 continued to press their attack, unloading a steady deluge of the insidious two-pound fire bombs upon the district. Every two and one half minutes, on the average, another bomber crossed the English coast and headed on a northerly course toward London. The raiders went unseen by ground spotters, but the Luftwaffe air crews could see their clearly illuminated target from a distance of many miles in spite of the heavy overcast.

Once they had reached the target area, the bomber pilots roamed at will. The anti-aircraft had picked up again, but was no more accurate tonight than it had been on any previous run. There had been warnings of night fighters; all eyes kept a sharp lookout for them, but none were spotted.

From a bomb-aimer's point of view, this was a dream mission. The sighting point, all lit up like a fiery lake, would have been difficult *not* to hit — even the very young and inexperienced crew members were finding it easier than they had expected. Some of the green crews released their bombs too early, but that kind of nervousness was an exception tonight. The bombardiers, prone on their stomachs over their bombsights, aimed carefully and took their time before releasing their payloads. The Heinkels and Junkers milled about until the bomb-aimer was content that each one of the Molotov Breadbaskets in the bomb bay would strike the lit up area below.

It was all very satisfying, knowing that their bombs were inflicting maximum damage. Not like on some raids, where they were never really sure if they were hitting their target or bombing some miserable fen a few miles away. The only problem was with turbulence — flying over the pillar of rising hot air buffeted the aircraft, lifting the whole plane upward for several hundred feet and then dipping it sharply down again.

The night was anything but satisfying to the Beaufighter and Hurricane pilots up looking for the intruders. So far, none of the Luftwaffe's aircraft had been shot down. Few of the raiders had been spotted, and fewer still had been approached to within firing distance.

The deck was stacked solidly against the RAF. The cloud layers hid the enemy from the sighting posts of the Observer Corps, leaving the fighters — especially the Hurricanes, with no radar — very much on their own. There was no moon to light up the bombers, so tracking the raiders would have to be done without any illumination or assistance from the ground. The fires, although bright enough to aid the Luftwaffe, were no help at all to the fighter pilots. All was frustration. London blazed brilliantly away within a few minutes' flying time, yet there was no sign of the enemy, right over the city and busily adding to those flames.

Besides the vital communications links at the General Post Office and Central Telegraph Exchange, Feldmarschall Sperrle's railway targets also had been hard hit. No trains ran within miles of Central London. Cannon Street and London Bridge railway stations were on fire; Waterloo Station flamed hotly, knocking out all platforms. When Guildhall's Control Centre was making its call to Redcross Street Station at 7.40 p.m., Fenchurch Street station, near the Tower, closed down because of damaged signals and debris-blocked tracks. Shortly afterward, Guildhall's phone room received another communication, a priority message from the Prime Minister, Winston Churchill — St Paul's Cathedral must be saved at all costs. Churchill's directive was passed on to St Paul's, but had little effect. Although the Prime Minister's concern was welcome and appreciated, there was little else for the Cathedral Watch to do that had not already been done.

From Number 10 Downing Street in Westminster, the flames within the City, lofting over the rooftops of Whitehall's War Office and Inigo Jones' Banqueting Hall, were lurid and frightening. 'All the sky were of fiery aspect, like the top of a burning oven, and the light seen above forth miles round about . . .' A description of another London blaze, in September 1666, is recalled by contemporary diarist John Evelyn.

God grant mine eyes may never behold the like, who now saw above ten thousand houses all in one flame, the noise and crackling and thunder of the impetuous flames, the shrieking . . . the hurry of people, the fall of towers, houses, and churches was like a hideous storm, and the air all about so hot and inflam'd that the last one was not able to approach it, and so they were forced to stand still and let the flames consume.

Civilian fire spotters often spelled the difference between survival and disaster, not only at St Paul's and Guildhall, but in office blocks and buildings throughout the fire ground. It is certain that most of the fires that now raged beyond control would never have got their death hold if more fire watchers had been on duty. Those on the job probably saved thousands of pounds of property each, single-handedly. But there were so few of them.

Sometimes one or two hearty souls would try to make up for the lack of fire spotters all by themselves. There was certainly nothing mundane about the activities of Benjamin W. Davis and his partner at W & D Harvest, Spices and Sundries Warehouse, in Dowgate Dock near Cannon Street Railway Station. With the reluctant aid of the overweight City policeman, these two had already saved Three Cranes Wharf from burning. Now they spotted a bomb that penetrated the roof of a nearby printing firm, Jarvis and Company.

This time, they knew better than to ask the corpulent police constable for help. Ben Davis and his partner went out and got the Fire Brigade's 'heavy gang' themselves, making much better time than during their last trip out. When the experts on breaking locks arrived from the fire station and broke into the printers' building, a glowering fire bomb was found smouldering away in the roofing.

Help from the outside was a rare thing, and when it did come, it was almost never in the right place or at the right time. Even the London Fire Brigade, lacking manpower and short of fire appliances, contributed its moments of frustration. Leonard Atkinson and the rest of the fire spotting crew at their Ludgate Hill Building Society had extinguished every fire bomb that fell on their roof — using full buckets of water, there had been, amazingly, no casualties. Now they had another source of danger to contend with. The building's water-proof paper window panes — replacing the glass panes that had been blasted out in an earlier air raid — had been set alight by the flaming building next door. Flames and burning embers from the adjacent blazing derelict entered the Building Society through these vacant windows and started outbreaks of fire. Before long, an entire section of the building was alight. The flames were more than the volunteer crew could deal with, so the men sent for the Fire Brigade.

A fire appliance arrived within a very short time after the call was made. The fire engine came to a stop in front of the Building Society, and its crew stepped down off the pump to take a good look at the blaze. They stood there in the street for a moment, gazing with clinical detachment. Suddenly, one of the firemen piped up, 'It's not nearly big enough yet — we'll be back later.' With that, the entire crew climbed back aboard their fire engine and drove off, giving Leonard Atkinson and his fellows their last glimpse of the London Fire Brigade for the rest of the night.

While Ludgate Hill fell prey to the rampaging flames, on Old Street, just north of the City Boundary, whole rows of buildings were already reduced to burnt-out hulks. Fire-weakened roofs collapsed inside buildings, releasing a sudden dazzling jet of orange or yellow flame and smoke. Death throes from within the walls rumbled out into the street. Falling beams and girders embedded themselves in floors or clanged heavily together, and debris rattled down from one burning floor to another. There was nothing that Stanley G. Champion and his partner Howard, the fire watchers at Jackson Brothers Ltd. at Number 47 Old Street, could do to save their firm. It had flames from top to bottom, along with its neighbours.

So the pair went to work assisting the Fire Brigade. The fire service was seriously short of men, and the two of them were promptly enlisted as runners, scurrying back and forth from Baltic Street Auxiliary Station with messages and requests.

Most of the City's main thoroughfares were choked with what seemed like miles of fire hose and heaps of glass and stone from the ruins all round. Fire appliances trying to make their way through these avenues – Queen Victoria Street; Cannon Street; Ludgate Hill; Upper Thames Street – were slowed to a walking pace; some roads were in danger of being blocked altogether. Many smaller streets were already sealed, making it impossible to get at the fires burning within them. If all this was not bad enough, a new conflagration had reached full bloom in the City's eastern end, in the Minories, north of the Tower.

In the thirteenth century, this street was occupied by the abbey of an order of Spanish nuns who called themselves the Sisters of St Claire, or *Sorores Minores*. Now the Minories was lined by a grim array of dingy, windowless warehouses, sulking at the City's eastern fringe just beyond the blitzed St Katherine's Dock area. Earlier on this night, the Minories had been hit by several clusters of fire bombs, but there was no one around to extinguish the flames while still small enough to control. Now the entire length of the Minories, a quarter mile stretch from Tower Hill to the north of Aldgate Pump, blazed furiously.

Everywhere, the fires still spread faster than anyone thought possible. The Fire Brigade did its best, but could not be everywhere at once. When Sub-Officer Richard B. Horne arrived at Gough Square, off Fleet Street, with his two heavy pumps, a major fire was already blazing away with no firemen in attendance. His crew quickly hooked up to the hydrant and ran out the hoses, but only a trickle of water ebbed out of the nozzles. At least they would not have to worry about stumbling about in the dark; the fires across the square were giving off plenty of light.

The upper floor of Dr Samuel Johnson's house, where the great man compiled his famous dictionary two hundred years before, was burning; Sub-Officer Horne sent some of his men across the square to attack the flames, using sand to smother them for want of water. The rest set to salvaging equipment from a burning factory building, which was the primary blaze in the square. The firemen kept on dragging property outside until chemicals, exploding under the intense heat, began giving off noxious fumes that nearly knocked Horne out.

A half mile to the east, Superintendent William E. Norwood, along with two other staff officers from Fire Brigade Headquarters in Lambeth, had established a control centre at the intersection of Aldersgate Street and Jewin Street. Headquarters had a direct line through to Redcross Street Fire Station, and had a good idea of the amplitude of the inferno. Superintendent Norwood had been sent out in the hopes of linking the fire appliances in the Barbican and Gresham Street with the pumps operating in Moorgate. This link-up would cut the City's western fire zone in half, isolating many of the more stubborn combustions and making them easier to take care of.

It did not take Superintendent Norwood and his two men long to discover that the situation was far worse than headquarters realised. Most of the roads were blocked by the remains of fallen buildings, making any sort of link-up impossible. When Superintendent Norwood informed headquarters, this complication, along with the other bad news — the non-existent water supply; the rapidly depleting 5,000 gallon emergency water tanks; and the radiated heat which turned narrow alleyways and courts into baking kilns — led to a change in tactics. The major effort would now be to keep the fires from spreading; there was no sense in throwing any more men and resources into that apparently bottomless pit of flame. Areas already out of control would be left to burn themselves out.

But none of the men working in the fire zone had any conception of a grand design or master strategy for fighting the conflagration; each crew had their own ordeal. Impaired vision was a peril suffered by everyone at some time. The shadowy red streets played tricks with the eyes. Heavy smoke sometimes blocked out all vision.

In the rose-coloured twilight, firemen tripped over straggling lengths of fire hose; falled beams and blocks of debris went unseen in the half-light. When a strong gust of wind sprang up, bits of flying embers would catch underneath the eyelids, causing painful burns and blinding the victim for several hours.

Fire Brigade officers could be another occupational hazard. Some officers used their rank the way a dockside bully uses a club, especially on members of the A F S. Auxiliary Fireman James Mayes' pump had been directed to a fire at a Lyons Tea Shop just off Aldersgate Street; when he arrived, the shop was already aglow with flame and on the verge of going beyond control. Mayes had only been there a few minutes when an LFB officer arrived and announced that he was taking charge. After a quick look at the situation, the officer ordered Mayes and the rest of his crew to drag a length of fire hose through a passageway that ran underneath the burning building. Mayes thought the order was suicidal — the place was already blazing hotly and getting worse by the second; it looked like it might collapse any time — but found himself hauling firehose toward the tea shop, with the officer in the lead.

They had just reached the beginning of the passageway when a pile of masonry and gutters came crashing down, striking Mayes on his helmet and making him stagger. A close call, but he would not have to worry about the job anymore; the cave-in had put an end to that. A quick glance told Mayes that the passage had been blocked off completely.

Since the beginning of the air raid two hours past, the number of people killed was miraculously light. Apart from the thirty

people killed instantly by an exploding bomb aboard Ron Woolaway's tram, there had been no multiple fatalities; the dead were
scattered singly throughout the Luftwaffe's target area. Feldmarschall Sperrle's decision to drop mainly incendiary bombs
was largely responsible for the low death toll so far — those
living or working within a fire-bombed building had ample time
to evacuate, but there was no running from 550 lb of bursting high
explosives.

Once in a while a person did not have enough time to run from
a fire either. On Wood Street Auxiliary Fireman E. Paltender was
buried alive when a calcined wall collapsed on top of him. Another
auxiliary was killed on Fleet Street and, on Tooley Street in
Southwark, Fireman E.V. Ainbridge suffered fatal wounds. Nor
were casualties confined to members of the Fire Brigade. In
Golden Lane a woman trapped in her cellar by falling beams,
was cremated when the blazing building above crashed into the
basement.

The fires were still being fought on a block-by-block, and even
an incident-by-incident, basis. High ranking L F B officers tried
vainly to organise some sort of overall campaign but, mainly
because of lack of communication to put together a systematic
attack, were failing. Reports from most of the local fire stations
were sketchy at best, and contacts with firemen on the spot were
almost non-existent. There was no such thing as radio contact,
and dispatch riders were few and far between. And usually, comments from the men were so vague that they were no use at all:
'Never saw so many fires in my life,' or, 'Bloody remarkable, those
flames.'

Regional Fire Officer Sir Aylmer Firebrace, at the Home Office
Fire Control Room in Whitehall, knew there was a crisis at hand
without any such reports — he had only to go out in the street to
see that — but had no exact details. So, Commander Firebrace,
accompanied by his senior staff officer A.P.L. Sullivan, left the
Home Office at about 7 p.m. to travel through the fire area and
size up the situation for himself.

A tall, ruddy-complexioned man, Commander Firebrace had
been in uniform for so many years that he looked and felt uncomfortable in civilian clothes. First as a naval officer and then

as an executive in the London Fire Brigade, Commander Firebrace had spent all of his adult life in the service. When the Blitz
began he had been the LFB's Chief of Fire Staff, but, earlier
in December, Home Secretary Herbert Morrison had invited Firebrace to join the Home Office staff.

In his new post as Regional Fire Officer, Commander Firebrace was in charge of moblising the many and varied provincial
fire brigades outside the hundred or so square miles under the
London County Council's jurisdiction. It was up to him to call
these units into London should they be required this night. For
this reason, Firebrace had to know specifically what problems
were shaping up regarding the fires: how fast the flames were
spreading; how many pumps were already on the scene; if additional
fire units were necessary, or would only be in the way. A personal look was the best way to find his answers. The first stop on
his fact-finding tour would be the mile-long stretch of flame in
Southwark.

Commander Firebrace and A.P.L. Sullivan drove across to the
Thames' South Bank, noticing from the roadway of the bridge
that the tide was out. Firebrace made a note that the low water
would make it impossible for the fire boats to come within range
of the inferno. The two officers visited the combustions in Borough
High Street, and the threatened London Bridge Station and Guy's
Hospital. Fires were developing everywhere along their route, and
at every stop, there was always the same complaint: not enough
experienced firemen on the job, and, usually, no water at all. After
an hour of watching things going from bad to worse, the two men
returned to the North Bank, re-crossing the Thames into the City.

Back on the northern shore, Firebrace and Sullivan soon discovered that the roadways were not fit for driving — the piled-high
debris in every street effectively blocked their car. They had
intended to drive up to Redcross Street Fire Station, but could go
no further than Cannon Street; from there, they had no choice but
to proceed on foot. While Feldmarschall Sperrle's bombers growled
overhead, the two fire officers started walking into the heart of
the inferno.

The way north from Cannon Street was brightly lit by blazing
buildings and alive with falling beams and glowing hot ashes. The

rubble that blocked their car now made walking almost impossible; Firebrace and Sullivan hopped from one great chunk of masonry to another, as though stepping across a swiftly moving stream. Several abandoned fire appliances were bypassed, completely burnt out and still smouldering, with their rubber tyres melted into a sticky mass from the hot asphalt. Commander Firebrace noted with professional efficiency that the situation was still deteriorating — he had no way of telling where or when the fires would eventually stop.

When the two reached Redcross Street Station, they found it surrounded by flames. Both sides of Redcross Street and the length of Jewin Street were rows of searing firebrands. The mediaeval church of St Giles, Cripplegate, directly across Redcross Street from the fire station, was a fiery wreck. The interior of the station offered even less encouragement. Kerosene lamps and candles lit the control room; the lights had been out for some time and the exchange lines were dying one one by one. The temperature was already uncomfortably warm and rising steadily.

Commander Firebrace and A.P.L. Sullivan held an emergency meeting with a few of the station's officers. The circumstances, they explained, were graver than any of them realised. It would only be a matter of an hour, perhaps less, Firebrace told the officers, before the station would have to be abandoned, a scrupulous prediction. A very short time later, after Sullivan and Firebrace had left, Redcross Street Station was evacuated. Firemen and firewomen trudged northward over the heaps left by destroyed buildings in Whitecross Street until they reached an air raid shelter; from the station, they jumped down onto the underground tracks of the Metropolitan Railway line. The tracks led the evacuees to the sanctuary of the Smithfield Central Market, beyond the flames.

After Commander Firebrace and A.P.L. Sullivan left Redcross Street Station, they continued their walking tour of the fire area. The two of them travelled east from Redcross Street along Fore Street; the blazing derelict buildings and helplessness of the fire crews they encountered reinforced their feelings of anxiety. If the flames were ever going to be stopped, it would be necessary to call in as many fire-fighting units as possible from the provinces. When the tide started coming in and relays from the Thames began pumping quantities of water into the area, every available man would be needed to combat the fires.

The two men continued along Fore Street until, at long last, they reached Moorgate and safety. In due course, they arrived back at the Home Office in Whitehall, where Commander Firebrace began calling the fire brigades of Essex, Kent, and Surrey into the London fire area.

The fierce fire inspired a variety of reactions in those not directly involved in fighting the flames. Nurse Marjorie Thyer's determined push toward University College Hospital had resumed its slow but steady pace. She had been joined by a helpful gentleman who was going in the same direction and, walking through the blacked-out streets, was very thankful for his company, especially since he insisted upon carrying her overnight case. The two steadily made their way toward the carmine light in the west — Nurse Thyer did not realise until later that she was walking along the Old Kent Road — while the anti-aircraft batteries kept up their incessant, ear-splitting chorus.

Curiosity and fear, sometimes a mixture of both, were the most common responses. Mrs G. Timbers and her husband were on their way from Balham to King's Cross railway station in one of the very few taxis out on the road, which two soldiers had offered to share with them. The barriers of flame seemed to close in on the taxi as the driver, displaying his very best 'business as usual' manner, nosed his way around road blocks and through City side streets. The driver of postman L.E. Benning's trolley bus, which was travelling toward East Ham, was afraid to go any further than Shoreditch, so Benning and another postman, his friend and co-worker, had to get out and walk the rest of the way. From the distance, Benning thought the fires were a lovely sight and only wished that they were fireworks. His partner shared his thoughts and, to Benning's annoyance, stopped to take in the view.

The excitement and unreal atmosphere produced by the block upon block of flame could make a person lose touch with reality. In the dreamlike red glow, awful, yet peculiarly intoxicating, everyday thoughts flew right out of a man's head. Special Constable R.E. Crowfoot had been walking about in the City for an hour, every since his trolley bus stopped at Old Street. He had seen the raging fires along Old Street and Fore Street, the buildings roaring furiously from inside, and spoke with firemen about the failed water pressure. While on Gresham Street, Crowfoot heard the muffled *crruummp* of high explosive bombs off to the east, and caught a good look at the fire fighting equipment on Cheapside. When he reached London Bridge Station, it suddenly dawned on him that his wife and family were getting worried about him; he should have arrived back at his house by this time. With this in mind, Crowfoot set out for home.

The beneath-the-surface anxiety of civilians within the City and Southwark was now giving way to alarm as the temperature of the air rose to fantastic heights. Shelterers who evacuated their places for a safer area often found themselves wishing that they had stayed where they were. The air outside was so hot that it made breathing painful, blinding embers wafted through space, and the pavement scorched their feet, making the rubber soles on shoes stick to the concrete. The night telephonists in the Faraday Building, just south-west of St. Paul's, were having an unpleasant time. Their building was a modern concrete structure and did not catch fire, but the air inside was smoky and fume-filled and stifling hot.

The ancients regarded fire with grave superstition, worshipping it with elaborate rituals and harsh taboos, and sought to appease it with living sacrifices. Anyone witnessing tonight's conflagrations could understand why. The fires were a living, breathing thing, moving with a life of their own, ravaging with Olympian dominance. Perhaps the primitives had something in their beliefs and superstitions, at that. The body of flame enveloping the ancient City consumed all in its path with the spiteful power of Homeric gods or devils from hell, overpowering and unstoppable.

By 8 p.m. the fires in Wood Street were past controlling. Shortly after the hour, the police ordered the staff at the Metropolitan Telephone Exchange to evacuate the building, on fire and surrounded by flaming ruins, and escorted the telephonists to St Paul's Underground Station, opposite the General Post Office. Another communications centre had been destroyed; Feldmarschall Sperrle's tally kept increasing. Gordon Papps and the roof

PHYPERS. V. COATES. R. JOHNSON. F. HARRIS. S. EMPSON. W. OAKMAN. E. WALDRON. J. MUTCH. J. ROBERTS. A. SANDERS. G. DOWNES. W. SH
J. RUNDLE. L. PARRISH. J. CAIE. W. SMITH. E. MOTT. F. BLANDFORD.

H. WALDEN. G. SARGEANT. J. WALKER. A. JEFFERY. N. ROLLIN. G. BUCKLE. F. HANCOCK. L. ALMOND. J. LANHAM. J. PARROTT. J. GUNSTONE. F. RO
J. O'RIORDAN. J. COCKS. W. G. JENKINS. F. LEAVER. C. ATKIN. H. WINTER. J. COFFIELD. A. BUCKHURST. S. GIBB. J. WILSON. C. FRISBY. C. RO
M. JENKINS. T. WILSON. E. GOSLING. W. WILLIAMS. S. HAWKINS.

ADAMS. T. CALNAN. R. HUGGINS. W. PINNER. D. COOPER. C. LADD. G. RIPLEY. S. HOOKER. S. HUME. R. S. KERR. A. PHIPPS. H. WILE
H. LESTER. R. LILLYCROP. M. CLARKE. F. FOSTER. R. SCHILLING. F. POCOCK.

Bottom Row. J. WRIGHT. S. EVANS. S. TAYLOR. D. JENKINS. H. MAYDWELL. N. HERBERT.

The firespotting crew of Hitchcock, Williams & Co. Ltd. 69/70 St Paul's Churchyard, 'only a few yards north of the Cathedral,' with St Paul's in the background.

spotters at Hitchcock, Williams & Company, at 69/70 St Paul's Churchyard, did not wait to be told to evacuate their blazing buildings. It was clear that there was nothing more they could do. But before they left, Mr Papps and his colleagues grabbed up all the company papers and ledgers they could carry and moved them to a safe place.

Stapley and Smith's warehouse, which had been blasted by an explosion earlier in the raid, was also a blazing wreck, along with almost every other building on Fore Street. The four members of the fire crew saw no point in staying around, and so they elected to take refuge in the Bank Underground station, one of London's 'deep' shelters which was packed to overflowing. Apart from the regular, every-night shelterers, a number of orphans from destroyed basement shelters in the area had also come in out of the blitz. Seventeen year-old R.C.H. Constable, from the Stapley and Smith crew, had not been down very long when he heard a police announcement advising people to leave the overcrowded Bank Underground station. Such a large crowd in that relatively small space was an invitation to all sorts of unpleasant possibilities. Constable boarded a train for King's Cross railway station; from there, he would make his way home.

Not everyone found it so easy to get out of the tube stations. When Mrs Violet Clarke's train reached Mansion House Underground station, the train lights failed and the guard called, 'Everybody out!' She and the other passengers started up the stairs for the surface, but before they reached the top a policeman told everyone to go back down again. Feeling trapped and vulnerable with the trains stalled and unable to leave the station, Mrs Clarke sat down on her suitcase and, along with everyone else, wondered what would happen next. (The trains started again in a short while and Mrs Clarke reached her home in Uxbridge, Middlesex without further incident.)

Twelve year-old S.E. Arthur was at Oxford Circus tube station, but had no plans to travel anywhere. He was sheltering in the station with his family and one hundred or so other people, and was as curious as everyone else about the commotion going on up above. It had been announced that no one would be allowed to leave the station, but young Mr Arthur had other ideas. After slipping past the station staff and wending his way through a maze of passages and stairways, he finally reached the top. He was spotted and ushered back down after about ten minutes, but not before he got his look at the terrible glare. Five year-old Janet Beeston, riding by the City in her father's Ford, also received an indelible picture of the fires. Nearly four decades later, she can still remember the scene of 'streets and streets of buildings alight' and firemen shouting to one another.

The inside of an underground station was not always as safe as everyone thought. At 8.15, a high-explosive bomb penetrated Westminster Underground station, killing three shelterers. A.R.P. records show that ten more were killed when a shelter in South-wark was hit. The big bombs also knocked out several water mains, besides the already damaged 24-inch City main — three 36 inch and a host of smaller lines were damaged. Only a handful of high explosives had been dropped up to now, but each had done more than its full measure of damage. As one woman said, 'They came down like they had eyes.' And this was only the first strike — Feldmarschall Sperrle planned to strike the target with yet another wave of bombers.

Hauptmann Friedrich Aschenbrenner alternated his glance from the instruments of his Heinkel He111 to the blackness beyond the bomber's glassed-in cockpit. He maintained a steady south—south-westerly course over the towns and villages of Brittany, heading toward the airfield at Vannes, Kampf Gruppe 100's home base, keeping the aircraft underneath the clouds so that he would be able to pick up the runway lights visually. Since the twenty radiobeam-directed Heinkels of KG100 had taken off from Vannes almost four hours before, the cloud cover had settled closer to the ground, forcing Aschenbrenner to within a few thousand feet of the trees and rooftops skimming below the bomber's underside. The Hauptmann was happy that he was going home then, while he could still enjoy good visibility, instead of a few hours later, when ground fog would cut the range of vision to nil and make a routine night landing a nail-biting adventure.

As soon as Hauptmann Aschenbrenner spotted Vannes' flare path, parallel lines of light illuminating the main runway, he began his descent. The other nineteen Heinkels of Kampf Gruppe 100 had already landed — as its commander, he remained over the target to observe the damage done by his 'Fire Raisers'; since he was the last to leave London, he would also be last to land. Aschenbrenner eased the control column forward and brought the throttles slowly back, letting the aircraft slide gently downward as it lost forward speed.

The flare path, straight ahead, was coming up to meet the aircraft — flaps down; undercarriage down; airspeed decreasing. With a bump and the screech of rubber tyres, the Heinkel touched the runway; Hauptmann Aschenbrenner cut the throttles. He taxied the bomber off the flight path, switching off both engines when the aircraft reached its revetment. After four physically cramped and emotionally tense hours in the pilot's seat, it was a welcome relief to climb down out of the aircraft and stretch his arms and legs. Before reporting for de-briefing, Aschenbrenner decided to go over to the officers' mess for a cup of coffee.

Somehow, the coffee always seemed better after returning from a sortie, even though it was no different than the brew he drank down during the day without giving it a second thought. Refreshed, Friedrich Aschenbrenner walked through the cold, damp December night toward the Control Office, where he would report to the airfield's Control Officer and tell his story of tonight's strike. Several pilots and crewmen were in the room when Aschenbrenner came in, including the rest of his own crew; some talked, some smoked, others just sat silently. The control officer was listening to the end of one man's report, but everyone rose to their feet when the Hauptmann entered. Aschenbrenner returned their greetings and sat down to wait his turn for interrogation.

It was not long before Hauptmann Aschenbrenner was himself seated before the Control Officer's desk. The man behind the desk listened with interest, missing nothing as Aschenbrenner spoke. The Hauptmann had already given a cryptic report by radio, but now he gave it again in detail, from the passing of the X-beam's primary signal to making the slow 180° turn for home.

The Luftwaffe control officer was pleased by Aschenbrenner's account. Kampf Gruppe 100's twenty Heinkels had given the rest of the strike force a good, bright aiming point. Tonight's attack would be a success regardless of the weather. He felt sure that KG100 would receive another glowing commendation from Reichsmarschall Hermann Göring in Berlin.

As soon as he finished his report, Hauptmann Friedrich Aschenbrenner left the Control Office. The weather outside the hut showed no sign of improving. The solid grey-white ceiling stretched as far as he could see in every direction. As the low clouds drifted across Brittany's peninsula, visibility would be cut to zero and rain would probably begin to fall before long. All in all, a good night for some uninterrupted sleep.

Whatever Paris decided to do about the second strike, KG100 would not be part of it. As pathfinder unit, they had already done their job. This suited Hauptmann Aschenbrenner perfectly; he was glad that he would not have to make another trip on this night.

# CHAPTER EIGHT

# 'You Really *Must* Come up and see the Fire . . .'
## 8.30pm – 10pm

The heat generated at the heart of the inferno was extraordinary. Flames and scorching air crumbled stone walls, caused asphalt roadways to burst into flame, and twisted steel girders like so much putty. Moorgate Underground station, in the City's western fire zone, was totally burnt out. Inside the station, the heat became so severe that some of the supporting beams buckled, and even the railway tracks were warped. All the aluminium fittings and the glass from the lights melted and ran down the walls, forming pools on the concrete platform.

A forceful updraft had been created by the intense heat, pulling air into the centre of the inferno to feed the raging mass and make it hotter still. This artificial wind blew burning embers onto buildings that were baked dry, starting more fires. The beginnings of a fire storm had been born.

The heat-engendered winds of such a phenomenon, brought on by temperatures of 1,000°F or more, were capable of reaching gale force within a very few minutes. Fierce gusts would then fan the conflagration until it became a great hellish avalanche of flame.

As things now stood, the fires were still too closely contained to induce a full-fledged fire storm, although the temperature was right. Also, the width of Moorgate's roadway was serving as a ready-made firebreak, and so far had stopped the flames from spreading eastward. But the strong wind that gusted from the south-west, and the fire bombs that kept pelting the area, might quickly change that.

Despite everything that had happened, and was still happening, some people insisted upon going through with their everyday routine, which sometimes brought them closer to disaster than they could have realised. Human nature is conditioned to resist

change and cling to daily ritual regardless of all obstacles —
including air raids. Milk tank driver H. Thomas had left Hounslow,
Middlesex at 7.30, on his nightly run through London to Bow,
out to the east. The falling bombs caused him no difficulty until
he reached the traffic light by Charing Cross Station on the
Victoria Embankment. While waiting for the light to turn green,
driver Thomas heard 'a mighty swish' followed a few seconds
later by the sound of something pelting his tanker — but no
explosion. He instantly decided not to wait for the green light.
He put his rig in gear and moved out for Blackfriars.

A few minutes later, Mr Thomas arrived at the head of Blackfriars Bridge. Even though everything in front of him flamed and
crackled, he still was resolved to take his tanker right through the
City, just like on every other night. He always drove straight along
Queen Victoria Street on his regular route. So Thomas shifted
gears and turned onto Queen Victoria Street, which was studded
with flaming buildings on both sides, and began driving eastward.

He had not gone far when a City policeman stopped him.
The policeman asked Thomas where he was going, and was told,
'Bow' — to East London directly through the fire zone.

'Not down here, you're not!' the constable declared, and
pointed off toward Mansion House, the Lord Mayor's official
residence. 'Look at that.'

Thomas looked where the policeman pointed, and saw the
facade of a fire-weakened building crash down into the street.
If the policeman had not stopped him, Thomas reckoned that he
would have been passing that building when it collapsed.

Most Londoners were not as unworried about the bombing
as Mr Thomas. All throughout London, people thought and talked
of little else than the brilliant light that bathed everything in
crimson. Civilians, as well as firemen, remembered the 7th/8th
September Docks raid, when the Luftwaffe returned to drop
loads of high explosives and 'stoke up' the raging fires. It seemed
like a good bet that the same thing would happen tonight; the
flames certainly offered a tempting enough target. At their Building
Society on Ludgate Hill, the possibility of a follow-up raid was the
major topic of conversation between Leonard Atkinson and the
other two roof-spotters.

Londoners were dead right in their hunch. The second wave was still scheduled, the weather in northern France notwithstanding. Feldmarschall Hugo Sperrle's order stood unchanged. The first attack had successfully bombed the target, and aircraft were still taking off right through the overcast on their way to London. The second wave was expected to do the same.

None of the pilots and crewmen who flew the He111s and Ju88s of Luftflotte 3 had any inkling of Feldmarschall Sperrle's second strike order. When they returned to their airfields, expecting the rest of the night to themselves, the men received a very nasty surprise.

Major Schulz-Hein of Kampfgeschader 51 had no more trouble in reaching the airfield at Melun than Hauptmann Friedrich Aschenbrenner did in landing at Vannes. The Major had flown under the clouds covering France, and had sighted the runway's flare path from a few miles off. When his Junkers was somewhere north of Paris, drops of rain began splattering against the glassed-in cockpit. He set the airplane down during a light but steady shower.

Major Schulz-Hein duly reported to the Control Officer to turn in his report of the bombing mission. In terse, laconic phrases, he described the keyhole bombing through the lit-up gap in the clouds. He had hit the target, he was sure of that, or at least had dropped his fire bombs on top of the fires that were already burning. If the 'Fire Raisers' of Kampf Gruppe 100 had missed their mark, then so had every other wing, since everybody was bombing on Hauptmann Aschenbrenner's beacon.

The Control Officer took note of everything, but was especially interested in the fact that the target was visible through the overcast sky. The 'glamour boys' of KG100 had done their job well.

After Schulz-Hein ended his account, the Control Officer spoke up. Another attack had been ordered for tonight, he told the Major. Schulz-Hein's Ju88 was to be re-armed and re-fuelled and sent off to London again.

The Major was dumbstruck by such an order. After a moment, he voiced his protest to the Control Officer. This was no weather for flying. It was already raining, and the clouds were getting heavier and closer to the ground all the time. There was no guarantee that he would be able to take off without crashing, much less return to an airfield he could not see.

But the Control Officer was not giving the orders, only passing them along. Headquarters had scheduled two sorties, he explained; only Feldmarschall Sperrle could countermand the order, and no such word had been received from Paris. There was still more than an hour before it would be time to take off again, the officer continued, plenty of time for a meal or a cup of coffee. The next wave would not begin taking off until the last elements of the first attack had left the ground: orders from Headquarters.

It was not just the weather that troubled Major Schulz-Hein, although that was the worst part. Also, there were physical limits that should be considered. He and his crew were tired after returning from a combat sortie. Everyone lacked the well-rested edge that flying a bomber over enemy territory required, especially on a night like this.

Outside the Control Room, a light rain was still falling, and looked as though it would continue for quite a while. There was nothing to anticipate except rain, fog, and decreasing visibility. On top of everything else, the major felt more like going to sleep for a week than taking his Junkers back to London. As he walked across the wet field, Schulz-Hein wondered if he would make it back from this flight.

The towering scarlet pillar, thrusting through the layer of cloud above London, could be seen from as far away as the French coast by the Luftwaffe's bomber crews. On the ground, the glow from the flames also was visible for many miles around. From his doorstep in Morden, Surrey, ten miles south of St Paul's, Charles Devall judged that the blaze must be in the City — it was certainly farther west than the dock fires last September. Derek Osborne could see the reddish light in Bishop's Stortford, Herefordshire, twenty-seven miles to the north.

Mrs Frances Hine often watched the air raids from her top window in Isleworth, Middlesex, eighteen miles to the west, but tonight's fires were the worst she had seen. As she watched the steady, rose-coloured glare in the east, Mrs Hine had second thoughts about taking her children into London to see the play

*Where the Rainbow Ends* tomorrow afternoon.

The size and scope of the inferno sometimes played tricks with a person's judgement, making the blaze seem closer than it was. Eric Stratford, in the Army and stationed at Ashford, Middlesex, could see a 'huge red glow hanging over London,' and worried that his parents were in danger. Actually, his mother and father lived several miles to the west of the fire zone, in Chiswick, but he was not able to tell which section of London was on fire. Stratford tried to think of some way to get to Chiswick, 'train, bus, or anything', but could not get off the post.

The favourite and most repeated phrase by eye-witnesses of the fire is, 'You could read a newspaper by it.' Reporter Hilde Marchant of the *Daily Express*, astonished at the sight of her shadow on the pavement, opened a newspaper to see if it really was bright enough to read by — she felt sure that someone would say that it was. By the flames of Ludgate Hill, she was able to make out every word on the printed page.

The Great Fire of September 1666 had destroyed 87 of London's parish churches in the four days while that inferno raged. In less than three hours on this night, more than twenty churches, most of which had been rebuilt by Christopher Wren after the Great Fire, were destroyed or badly damaged.

The wooden roofs of these old buildings made them into fire-traps; bursting fire bombs set them ablaze almost instantly. Since there were no firewatchers on duty, the flames darted across the roofing boards unimpaired. It did not take long until the entire length and breadth flamed and crackled. When the supporting beams burned away, the vaulting crashed inside with a sickening roar, setting the pews and furniture on fire.

With the roof burnt away and all the windows gone, a steady flow of hot air rushed through the interior. The four free-standing walls, directing the air flow and feeding the burning beams, acted like a chimney, raising the temperature to the intensity of a furnace — or, more exactly, a crematorium. The mortal remains of the high-born and powerful that rested within the City churches, both famous and infamous, passed into extinction. Their bones, calcined by the flames, perished along with everything around them.

"After more than 100 nights of the Blitz, the shelter routine was partly habit and partly instinct." One of the thousands of public air raid shelters — this one in Trafalgar Square — throughout London.

"... people brought their bedding with them and slept on the cement platform." Londoners prepare to spend another night below ground in an Underground station. Many people not only slept in the "tube," but actually formed their own miniature societies. Note the suitcases that separate the sleepers on the left of the platform from the women talking under the poster.

Beneath the floor of St Giles Cripplegate, the bones of Sir Martin Frobisher, the Elizabethan explorer and commander, and the poet of *Paradise Lost*, John Milton, passed into dust. Inside Christchurch, Greyfriars, on Newgate Street, the remains of Edward II's implacable Queen Isabella, the 'She-Wolf of France', were obliterated. The skeleton of Judge George Jeffreys, the cruel and unjust 'Hanging Judge' who condemned hundreds of men to the gallows in the 1680s, became a handful of ashes. Although not all of these had died violently, all had lived and died during violent times. The way in which their last vestiges perished was, at least, in keeping with their eras. But with every monument that was destroyed, London lost another link with her past.

At Guildhall, matters took a sudden turn for the worse. The church spire of St Lawrence Jewry had been reduced to a weak and unstable wreck by the flames that had been devouring it for over an hour. While Guildhall's volunteer fire squad looked on, the blazing steeple fell back onto the church itself. Within minutes, the entire building was burning. The high winds fanned the flames, turning the church roof into a bonfire and sending a storm of burning ashes onto Guildhall's roof. These embers were immediately tackled by the fire crew, which sprayed the wooden roof with their stirrup pumps.

Buildings in and around the fire ground were being evacuated by the score, not only because of the dangers that already existed, but also with an eye toward the future — everyone expected the Luftwaffe to come back later. John Hyman and his family, along with the rest of the residents in their blocks of flats in Shoreditch, north-east of Liverpool Street Station, were moved to nearby Shoreditch Church to sit out the rest of the attack in the crypt. An Air Raid Warden escorted the families to the church. The warden kept everyone close to buildings to shield against flying shrapnel from anti-aircraft shells, and was especially careful to use his most casual tone of voice to avert panic. John Hyman suffered from an eye disorder that limited his vision in the blackout, but he had no trouble tonight. It was as bright as day; he could see as well as if it were afternoon.

The party reached Shoreditch Church without incident and began to settle down for the night. John Hyman did not mind the crypt very much. The vicar was a cheerful enough fellow; he organised a sing-song to keep up morale and to drown out the noise from outside. Mrs Hyman, however, did not like it at all. It was pitch dark except for the feeble torch beams of her fellow inmates, not very comfortable, and the constant warning, 'Don't take up too much space!' was disconcerting. But most of all she worried about her husband, who had such trouble seeing in the darkness. The men and women were kept on separate sides of the crypt, and she could not get across to visit him all night.

When the fire watchers at Hitchcock, Williams & Co., at 69/70 St Paul's Churchyard, evacuated their building, they set out for the crypt of a somewhat larger church — St Paul's Cathedral. Gordon Papps found the crypt interior eerie, not only because of the silence but also for the atmosphere in general. He spent the night sleeping on the grave of Sir George Williams, who had co-founded the firm in 1853, wrapped in a fur coat which he had rescued from the burning building.

The stillness of the crypt was a marked contrast to the upheaval boiling just outside. There were other refugees in the crypt as well, mostly from nearby shelters, all of whom came under the authority of George Garwood. Mr Garwood had taken a fall and hurt himself earlier on; since his fall, he had been looking after things in general inside the cathedral. The arrival of the shelterers gave him the additional job of bedding the new arrivals down and seeing that they had hot drinks. Most of the shelterers were, if not right at home, at least comfortable. One young lady decided to do a bit of sightseeing, buttonholing a clergyman with persistent questions about the Duke of Wellington's funeral carriage, which stood nearby.

Some people were having anything but a quiet time. The few travellers trying to make their way through the air raid were still fighting an uphill battle, although they made slow but steady progress. Nurse Marjorie Thyer finally realised where she was as she walked closer to the fire zone — the dome of St Paul's was the most brightly lit landmark for miles around. Now that she had got her bearings she had another unpleasant thought. She was completely off her usual route, and could not help thinking that if anything should happen to her now, no one would ever know.

Railway passengers were being dumped off at various places, left to fend for themselves. L.C. Roberts' journey from Farnborough, Hampshire, to Waterloo Station reached an abrupt end at Wimbledon. The train quickly emptied, but when the passengers climbed down the long stairway to the Underground, they found the station closed. The crowd began to pile into the narrow passageway. People were shoved on top of one another, the exits were blocked, and panic began to set in. Roberts still does not remember how he got out.

The underground trains were still running from King's Cross railway station, to the immense relief of Mrs G. Timbers and her husband. They got out of their taxi, said good-bye to their two soldier companions, and headed for the underground platforms.

When they reached the tube station, Mrs Timbers received the shock of her life. She had read about the people who slept in the Underground, but this was the first time she had seen them for herself. For months afterward she would be haunted by the closely huddled bodies, crammed together with hardly a space between them, and especially by the grotesquely white faces that stared out at her like spectres from a nightmare.

Milk tank driver H. Thomas was still trying to get out of the City. He had turned his tanker around and headed along Cannon Street, past St Paul's; after he passed the cathedral, Mr Thomas heard another 'terrific swish' and a dull thud and braced himself for an explosion, but there was none. A jam of fire engines near Mansion House forced him to come to a stop.

While he was sitting in his cab, another City policeman came over to speak to him. The constable told Thomas that most of the roads leading out of the City were blocked, but went on to suggest that he take a chance and head for Aldgate, which might still be open. Thomas took the suggestion. Driving around scores of pumps and over miles of fire hose, he made it to Aldgate and was soon on his way toward Bow, out of the fire zone.

At about the same time, fire appliances from all over Greater London were on every main road heading into the blazing district. In scattered boroughs and suburbs throughout the London County Council's hundred or so square mile jurisdiction, fire stations had already received the call they had been waiting for. From as close by as the West End to Barnes and Mortlake on the South Bank, regular firemen and auxiliaries were given their instructions. Singly, or in twos and threes, the fire appliances, mostly trailer pumps towed by automobiles, started off toward their assigned destinations.

It was about 9 p.m. when Edward Kelcey, of the Barnes Auxiliary Fire Service, was called out. He arrived at St Paul's Churchyard to find the entire area alight, while the Luftwaffe continued dropping their clusters of glittering incendiaries. Kelcey spotted an incendiary bomb as it hit Paulson and Lee's textile warehouse, and watched as the bomb burned its way through the entire building, floor by floor, until the whole place flamed 'like a great bloody haystack'. All the hydrants were dry, so the army began bringing up 500 gallon dams on flat-bed lorries. But this small supply was very quickly used up by the fire pumps; even the Coventry Climax trailer pumps used up to 150 gallons per minute.

The Hendon Auxiliary Fire Service, of north-west London, also got their call at about 9 p.m. Auxiliary Fireman E. Geoffrey Mosely's unit consisted of a Coventry Climax trailer pump, which was towed by a grand and luxurious Humber Snipe limousine. The luxury did not extend as far as an electric starter, however, and one of the crew would always have to crank the car to get it running.

The eight mile journey from Hendon was uneventful until the unit drove past St Paul's, when one of the trailer pump's jacks snagged a strung-out fire hose. The firemen who had laid the hose were not at all pleased, and roundly cursed Mosely and his crew for the inconvenience. As soon as the pump had been untangled, a Fire Brigade officer approached and directed the crew to the Central Telegraph Exchange on Wood Street. The officer apparently had not heard of the directive from Fire Brigade Headquarters, which dictated that the district be left to burn itself out.

Auxiliary Fireman Mosely and his crew managed to reach Wood Street, but could not gain entrance — the road was piled high with rubble from ruined buildings. Undaunted, they kept going until they reached Fore Street, where everything on both sides of the street was blazing. The rest of the crew ran out the hoses while Mosely, the pump man, found a hydrant and connected up — dry.

As he stood next to the useless hydrant, Mosely could see spades, forks, and other tools silhouetted against the flaming interior of a windowless ironmonger's shop.

The problems caused by water pressure did not always involve dead hydrants. Auxiliary Fireman James Mayes had been fighting the blaze in the Lyons tea shop near Aldersgate Street for over an hour. His pump was being fed by a 5,000 gallon static water dam near Aldersgate Street, and had an adequate supply of water. The crew put the nozzle of the fire hose in a Branch Holder, a device that gripped the hose and kept it trained toward the fire, which allowed them to boost pressure as well as to take a rest. Mayes and his cronies kept moving the branch, shifting the jet of water from place to place, which is probably what caused the clip on the branch holder to break.

The fire hose whipped out of control, its heavy brass nozzle snapping in all directions. Mayes dived flat on the ground and everyone else scurried for cover to escape the flapping bludgeon, which could break a man's skull or fracture an arm. Finally, one of the crewmen saw his chance and ran to the pump, shutting off the water and averting what might have been a costly accident.

By 9 p.m. the Fire Brigade had already arrived at St Lawrence Jewry's Church, which was burning furiously. After looking it over for a minute or so, the firemen decided to tackle the blaze from Guildhall's roof.

The roof of Guildhall had several small outbreaks of fire itself, caused by sparks which flew over from the flaming church. The volunteer fire squad was dispatched to put out these combustions and to spray any exposed wooden sills with water from their stirrup pumps. One of the men, Fireguard R.C.M. Fitzhugh, was sent to report that the Fire Brigade had arrived. When he reached the Great Hall, Fitzhugh was astonished to discover that fires had also broken out *inside* the building. But the flames were minor, so it came as a surprise that so many men — the regulars of the Fire Brigade and the local AFS as well as Guildhall's volunteers — had been called in to deal with these seemingly insignificant flames. He thought they would be better put to use elsewhere.

At airfields all across northern France — Orly, Tours, Etampes,

St André-de-L'Eure — the weather continued to thicken. The bombers of each Kampfgruppe kept landing one at a time; each aircraft that set down had a bit more difficulty than the one that landed before. A steady rain was now falling on the southernmost airfields, making the runways slick and wet. While taxiing to a stop, the bombers would jar slightly as they rushed through a puddle.

In wet weather these airfields rapidly became unserviceable. Very few had paved taxiing lanes; most air bases had only dirt runways and revetments. During the rainy winter months, the runways became soggy stretches of soft mud, unable to support the twin-engined Heinkels and Junkers. Take-offs with full bomb loads were hazardous at best under such conditions, even if the decreasing visibility was not taken into account. Operations usually were brought to a standstill.

When the pilots and crews of Luftflotte 3's Gruppen were informed of the second strike, reactions were as varied as the men themselves. Most received the order stolidly, with no outward show, knowing that it would do no good to protest at Headquarters' decision. Some cursed out loud. Others refused to believe it: nobody would be taking off in this weather, orders or no orders. In another hour, when they were supposed to take off, the runway would be a river of mud. Even Headquarters could not stop the rain.

But there had been no official word to halt the sortie. As far as anyone could tell, Feldmarschall Sperrle still planned on going through with it.

Some of the men who had been forecasting a cancellation of the mission were now having second thoughts about their predictions. Maybe the brass hats in Paris knew something that they did not — the meteorologists had their trade secrets, and always seemed to have an ace up their sleeve. This might just be a front passing through; by take-off time, the rain have stopped. The sky over London might well be clear already, and in an hour or so the storm front could have broken up. Looking through the windows of their huts at the rain and grey-white clouds, none of the airmen, however, could see how.

The sky over London was anything but clear. Luftflotte 3's

pilots and crewmen looked down upon the same endless clouds that Kampf Gruppe 100 had skimmed three hours before. There was only one gap in the carpet of overcast — the several square-mile hole that the fires beneath had burned through it. The Heinkels and Junkers swarmed toward this lit-up beacon like so many dark, droning insects. Singly, they flew in, released their bombs, and turned for home again.

Anti-aircraft fire was still heavy, but the guns continued to shoot low by thousands of feet. Over the target, however, even the brightly bursting flak shells failed to hold the airmen's attention. The flames below, brighter and more lurid than anyone expected, demanded single-minded concentration. A great column of smoke, stained red by the fires, met the bombers even at an altitude of 14,000 feet. Flying time over the target was only a few seconds duration, but the inferno, with its sharply etched boundaries, left an indelible impression in the mind's eye.

After 'bombs gone' and the short, bumpy ride over the updraft, the navigator set course for home base. Nobody said much about what they had seen, at first. Afterward, when the shock had worn off, there would be a great deal of talk about the brilliant fires and the clouds of smoke, but for now the impact was too immediate.

Despite the falling bombs and the steady rain of anti-aircraft shrapnel, people all over London were stopping whatever they were doing and going outside for a better look at the violently beautiful flames. Those in and near the City and Southwark did not have the Luftwaffe's sweeping vista, but were none the less impressed by what they saw.

From their rooftop in Dowgate Dock, close by Cannon Street Station, Benjamin Davis and his partner had a superb view of the blaze. A short distance from their post, a warehouse filled with Brasso metal polish roared 'like a blast furnace' in a rage of white-hot flames. Another warehouse on Cannon Street had been reduced to a red-hot steel skeleton; the squared framework reminded Davis of a huge brazier. In spite of their rooftop view, the two of them decided to go down to the street to see how things looked from there.

The outlook from ground level was a lot different than from the roof. The panoramic view might have been awe-inspiring, but the continuous wall of fire and noise was much more graphic. They only had to walk a little way to be surrounded by flaring hulks of warehouses and office blocks. When Ben Davis went to light a cigarette, he was surprised when a policeman ordered him to get under cover before striking a match — he was violating the black-out.

In Hornsey, north London, where E.R. Cooke was visiting his parents, the crimson aura was clearly visible. Mr Cooke's father, a window cleaner, got out one of his extension ladders and they climbed up on the roof to watch the inferno. Because of the S-bend in the Thames, Mrs Phyllis Fisher, living in Mulberry Walk, Chelsea, thought that the great fire was on the South Bank. When she went up on her roof to spot fallen fire bombs, she could see the dome of St Paul's silhouetted against the blaze. The sky was incandescent with red and orange that seemed to tower miles into the air. Mrs Fisher was sure that this was the last she would ever see of St Paul's.

Mrs Gwladys Cox, listening to the radio in her flat at Cholmley Gardens, Hampstead, about five miles north of the fire ground, was interrupted by a knock at the door. When she opened the door, an upstairs neighbour excitedly whispered from the darkened hallway,

'You really *must* come up and see the fire from our windows — the whole City of London seems burning.'

Mrs Cox recorded the episode in her diary:

So we went upstairs and, from their top floor window, facing south-east, with its wide, uninterrupted view of London away to the East End, we watched . . . a spectacle of the most terrible beauty I have ever witnessed.

It was a dark and moonless night and the whole sky to the east, above the City, was a vivid sheet of flame . . . we realised at once that the conflagration centred round St Paul's . . . volumes of rose-pink smoke and many-coloured flashes from explosions pierced again and again the blood-red clouds which, brooding and angry, hung for miles over the City.

Once again, Samuel Pepys' description of the 1666 Fire is recalled:

> . . . how horribly the sky looks, all on a fire in the night, was enough to put us out of our wits. And indeed it was extremely dreadful, for it looks just as if it were at us, and the whole heaven on fire.

From a distance the fire seemed to be a great mass of red flame, but firemen and roof spotters saw a myriad of colours in the heart of the inferno. Each ignited building radiated its own peculiar colour, depending upon what was burning inside. Chemicals gave off a very hot white or yellow flame. Wooden packing crates, as well as furniture and bedding, burned bright vermilion, while rubber blazed a dull, deep red and emitted clouds of black smoke. From rooftops and turntable ladders a great, terrifying kaleidoscope met the eye.

Sub-Officer Sid Willmott had been operating a turntable ladder unit in the Barbican, the street with the ancient Roman name, for about an hour. One of his men was up on the end of a 100-foot ladder, hosing down a tall building that was 'going well' and describing the view from up there into the telephone mouthpiece. The ladder man had been up for quite a while, so Willmot told him to fix the branch on the fire and come down for a breather. When the ladder man climbed down, Willmot went up to take his place.

Now it was Sub-Officer Willmott's turn to describe the scene. The heat was overpowering and great beads of sweat trickled down from under his tin hat, but the sight of the raging conflagration took his mind off the temperature. The fires stretched along Fore Street as far as Finsbury Circus and as far south as the Thames. He remembered the famous over-excited radio commentator who described King George VI's light-bedecked Coronation Naval Review at Spithead three years before with, 'The whole bloody fleet's lit up!' On the telephone to his crew one hundred feet below, Willmott could not resist proclaiming, 'The whole bloody town's lit up!'

The thousands of separate fires that made up the great inferno did not always burn with a single-coloured flame, but changed their tints as the wind gusted or changed direction. A rainbow of shades, some almost delicately radiant, transfixed onlookers — deep crimson flecked with scarlet; blue tinted with yellow-green; vermilion edged by orange and gold — all tossing in the north-easterly gale.

Each district was floodlit by its own particular tincture. Cheapside, by St Martin-le Grand, was lit up in bright orange, while the south and east sides of St Paul's Cathedral were bathed in pale apple-green. The fire watchers at Guy's Hospital, Southwark, were surrounded by white flames. R.C.H. Constable, walking from King's Cross railway station to Liverpool Street Station, saw predominantly yellow reflected in the overhanging smoke. Every once in a while, a new crop of incendiaries would clatter down, enveloping the immediate vicinity in stark blue-white. The overall effect was of an other-worldly nightmare will o' the wisp, a carnival night in hell.

An atmosphere of primaeval madness prevailed. Everything seemed grotesque and unearthly. The light and excitement created by the great multi-tinted furnace bred strange thoughts in the minds of spectators. To fifteen year-old Dorothy Harms, living near City Road, the whole scene was like a dream: the fire and smoke, the unholy glow, and the noise of the fire pumps and anti-aircraft guns seemed too lurid to be real.

More than one fireman, staring into the dazzlingly brilliant wall of flame, suffered a sensory breakdown — a revolt of the senses brought on by the spectacle only a few paces in front of them. Some were literally hypnotised, unable to take their eyes away from the flames. Others experienced mild hallucinations, seeing weird forms and unreal faces in the wind-blown fires. Even other firemen, when seen in that half-light, looked like strange creatures from another world.

Sometimes, all the excitement only served to heighten a person's natural exuberance. Auxiliary Fireman Edward Kelcey had to knock down the door to get at the flames inside a Lyons Tea Shop near Ave Maria Lane. He had never used his fire axe before, and thoroughly enjoyed chopping down the wooden door. Inside, he found the chairs neatly stacked on top of the tables, but they did not stay that way for long. Kelcey was having the time of his life

"... so wide and deep that the Royal Engineers would have to build a bridge across it." Two weeks after the City Fire Blitz, a bomb blew this gigantic crater in front of the Royal Exchange.

wrecking the tidy arrangement with the pressurised jet from his fire hose, and watching the chairs fly about like tenpins.

Sometime shortly after Auxiliary Fireman Kelcey had axed his way through the tea shop's door, Guildhall's luck finally ran out. The ancient meeting hall, which had remained almost miraculously undamaged even though hemmed in by fires on all sides, began to burn.

The wind-blown embers from the blazing church of St Lawrence Jewry had set the hall's wooden roofing beams on fire. The roof fires spread quickly along the inside of the hall, aided by the gale force winds that whistled through the rafters. Fireguard R.C.M. Fitzhugh, who had been surprised that so many men had been called in to deal with the flames, was astonished to find that none of the firemen had done anything about them. When he asked one of them what was wrong, he was told that there was no water. The Fire Brigade had been ready for fifteen minutes, but could do little except watch the flames crawl maddeningly along the wooden beams.

John Murphy, the City of London's Air Raid Precautions Officer, left Guildhall's control room to see for himself how things were progressing. By the light of the fires all around he could see a great many fire hoses pointed toward the roof but only a faint trickle of water ran from the nozzles.

It seemed that everything was going wrong. As the flames spread and fanned out, the high winds whipped them along with alarming deftness. Glowing bits of ash blew into other parts of the Guildhall complex, coming in through roof ventilators and windows. Firemen did their best to jack up the water pressure with their pumps, but the spray still would not reach the roof. The Fire Brigade next tried to bring a mobile water tower within range, but the appliance was too large to fit through the yard entrance. Several members of Guildhall's own volunteer fire squad moved precariously along the gabled roof with fire buckets — balancing a bucket in each hand — to drown the billowing flames. It was a feeble attempt, but it was the best that could be done by anyone.

The telephone operators down in Guildhall's control room were well out of noise range, and were not aware that the building was

in any immediate danger. Sub-Officer Frank Lawrence was heed-
less of the activity going on all around, and had no idea that the
hall was on fire until he was told by a member of the staff.

By 9.50, the fires were out of control. The Great Hall's peaked
wooden roof blazed angrily, and it looked as though the entire
building would be a roaring inferno before long. Aware of the
gravity of the situation, Fireguard Joseph E. Burt returned to
headquarters to rescue the building's only set of keys. He cut
through the canteen along the way, and found the place burning
steadily. Wartime rationing had made food a rare and precious
commodity; almost everything was hard to come by. Rather than
have the canteen's supplies go up in flames, Burt decided to salvage as much food as he could carry from the room.

The attack showed no sign of ending. Flight after flight of
Luftwaffe raiders droned steadily over the southern home counties
on their way to London. Eileen McConville thought that every
aircraft in Germany was following her during her twenty minute
uphill walk from the railway station in Ewell, Surrey, to her
home. When she reached the house, she found her mother and her
dog up waiting for her. Her father had an early Monday call and
was in bed, sleeping right through the noise.

# CHAPTER NINE

# "You Aren't Going to Charge these Firemen Anything . . . Are you?'
## *10pm – 11.40pm*

Feldmarschall Hugo Sperrle received one piece of bad news after another. Every one of Luftflotte 3's bases reported deteriorating weather conditions — indeed, it was raining outside Sperrle's own window at the Hotel Luxembourg in Paris — and staff meteorologists were predicting no end to heavy weather for at least twenty-four hours.

Normally, Sperrle would have had no qualms over calling off the second strike. He had not been overjoyed at sending his Heinkels and Junkers to London tonight in the first place. One of Sperrle's main concern during every mission was with visibility — he wanted to be sure that his pilots and bomb-aimers would be able to see their target clearly. The reports of increasing cloud usually would have brought an immediate cancellation order from the Feldmarschall.

The news of the attack itself, however, was nothing but good. Every dispatch mentioned fierce, bright fires in the target area. Because the fire raid had been such a success, Sperrle was unwilling to cancel the second wave. The vivid fires would allow the bombers to find their aiming point in spite of the cloud layer and, since the flames were concentrated in and around the City district, the loads of high-explosive bombs would inflict maximum damage. Feldmarschall Sperrle had no intention of abandoning the follow-up attack.

In view of the weather over the Continent, however, the Feldmarschall decided that it might be wise to postpone the strike for a few hours. After this brief rollback, the second attack would still be able to bomb while the London fires burned brightly. Also, all units, even the very last squadrons, would be able to return to base under cover of darkness, before the day fighters were up. The heavy clouds might even ground the Spitfires and Hurricanes, giving the bombers even more margin for error.

Feldmarschall Sperrle gave his decision to his Chief of Staff, and the order was quickly sent out to all airfields: stand down.

The postponement did little to calm the nerves of Luftflotte 3's pilots and crewmen. Taking off an hour or two later would not make any difference. The runways would still be just as muddy, even if the rain did stop. And if the RAF fighters caught them after sunrise, many of them would never live to see Germany again. If anything, Feldmarschall Sperrle's order made everyone more tense than ever.

Just as Feldmarschall Sperrle's reports had indicated, the great fire on the North Bank was still concentrated, although it was still spreading relentlessly. The high winds continually drove the conflagrations, pushing them toward the north and east. At Lloyds Bank Buildings, 55/61 Moorgate, housekeeper J.C. Walsby was told to get ready to abandon the premises. Over 500 gallons of fuel oil were stored under the basement, fuel for the central heating system, and it was best not to take chances. But the flames did not come within threatening range and Mr Walsby, along with his wife and two children, remained in their basement shelter.

Not very many places were spared from the combined fury of the gale and the flames. By 10.10, Guildhall was flaming angrily. The hall had played a central role in the history of the City of London for over five hundred years. Now the Great Hall once again shared the City's fate, just as it had done during the Great Fire of 1666.

Along with the rest of the 'square mile', Guildhall was a victim of the high winds and the failed water supply. Hot smoke and burning chips were swept into the rooms and offices by the high winds, and the library caught fire. The rumbling of the wind-swept flames and dry crackle from the burning beams and roof timbers were loud enough to drown the voices of the firemen who still stood, helpless and frustrated, out in the street with dry fire hoses.

When the lights went out at 6.45, they were never switched on in the Great Hall. The only illumination in the ancient meeting hall came from the flames that were efficiently consuming the roofing beams and the raging flames that surrounded the Guildhall complex on all sides. The light outside the west windows, facing Aldermanbury, was so bright that the coloured figures in the stained glass were blotted out. Only the tracery stood out darkly in the fierce glow.

The telephonists in the control centre stayed on the job. Exchange lines were dying one at a time, but the operators continued to take incoming calls on the few remaining lines. The log book for this last Sunday of 1940 supplies a cryptic, tersely graphic account of the City's ordeal, giving the time and nature of each incident, and type of bomb involved. 'IB-F' signifies 'incendiary bomb-fire'.

| *call*: No 1 | 6.20 | Knightrider St. — Queen Victoria St. | IB-F |
| No 59 | 6.45 | Eastcheap by Mark Lane 'Explosive IBs are bursting all over the place.' | IB-F |
| No 62 | 6.59 | Queen Street by Mark Lane 'Well alight' | IB-F |
| No 74b | 8.10 | YMCA Bldg., 186 Aldersgate Street 'Fire spreading rapidly — nobody in building' | IB-F |
| No 137 | 9.10 | 26/27 Bush Lane 'LFB wanted *urgently*' | IB-F |
| No 171 | 10.00 | 12/16 Red Lion Court 'LFS in attendance, but no water' | IB-F |

The logbook records only a fraction of the over fourteen hundred fires in and around the City. This was partly because of Guildhall's overburdened telephones, which were swamped with calls for as long as the lines remained open, but mostly because so few people were in the district — there was no one about who could report the outbreaks.

The telephonists kept the lines open for as long as possible, but by 10.30 p.m. it was evident that the building would have to be abandoned. Before leaving, members of Guildhall's fire squad decided to save as much as they could carry from the museum and records department. The museum contained a number of valuable prints, and the records on file went back for several centuries, too valuable to be left to the advancing flames. On one of the salvaging forays, Captain S.E. Daw even had time to rescue the Town Clerk's wig. Everything was transferred to the two-storey strong room, which was much more resistant to flame than the storage rooms.

Charles Sone, attached to the Civil Defence Control Centre in Upper Thames Street, was despatched to help rescue the ancient papers and manuscripts. At Guildhall, he was assigned to a crew that was salvaging the books, and soon found himself passing volumes upstairs one at a time by means of a rope-pulley system. One book, a heavy, antiquated edition bound by padlocks, caught his attention. Sone opened it and began reading. It was all about Cheapside during the sixteenth century, and was so absorbing that Sone forgot all about the job at hand. An exasperated shout from above brought him back to reality: 'What about that other book? How about sending it up so we can get out of here?' He promptly sent up the volume and, his job finished, left the building. From the street, he could see the roof of the Great Hall blazing brightly.

By this time, only one telephone was still in operation. Sub-Officer Frank Lawrence could see no point in having his telephone operators stay inside the burning building any longer. He ordered the girls to leave Guildhall, telling them that there was nothing more for them to do.

The only way out was toward the south, to City of London Police Headquarters in the Old Jewry. Everything in all other directions crackled and flared hideously. It was all terrifying, but at the same time the scene was almost hypnotic. The evacuees stood speechless in the surrealistic glow, not able to move away from the most fantastic spectacle they had ever seen.

Although Guildhall burned, most of the historic papers and artefacts had been saved. Even more important, not a single life had been lost in the fire.

Nearly everyone had their own pet phobia about the fires. For some, it was the lurid glare. For others, it was the smoke and noise. For Richard Howlett, a stretcher bearer with the City of London Civil Defence, the worst part was sitting and waiting. He and his crew had been sent to the *Evening Standard* building on

Shoe Lane, where they sat with stretchers, splints, blankets, and bandages at the ready. But there was nothing for them to do, so they just stayed inside the car, feeling 'like sitting targets'. Howlett was relieved that his driver was hard of hearing – at least the racket of the guns and fires would not send him panicking.

Casualties from the air raid were still astonishingly light, although the death toll was climbing. If Richard Howlett and his crew had arrived in Shoe Lane a little earlier, they would have had plenty to do. Only a few hundred yards from where they now sat, Auxiliary Fireman S.N. Holden had been buried by a collapsing wall, and others had been injured.

Four more Auxiliaries had been killed when a fire-weakened wall in Islington fell directly on them. More civilians had been killed than firemen. Nearly one hundred had died so far, either trapped inside burning shelters or killed outright by exploding bombs.

Just south of the Thames, the Borough of Southwark had its own casualties, besides an abundance of fire outbreaks. Seventy-eight fire calls had been issued between 6.15 and 9.30, although Southwark's story was essentially the same as the City's – many more incidents had taken place, but there was no one to report them.

The gale force winds that were fanning the flames and causing so much damage in the City and Islington had, ironically, spared Southwark from more widespread damage. The wind blew the flames toward the river, away from the houses and flats off to the south. Also, good luck played a part. Many of the fire bombs that landed in the district inflicted only minor damage, while about one-third of the reported incendiaries burned themselves out on the pavement.

Evacuees from shelters and fire-wasted buildings on both sides of the Thames were evacuated to safer lodgings, taken in tow by Air Raid Wardens, usually to places outside the fire zone. But these overnight refugees were not the only people walking about in the middle of the attack. A number of travellers, grimly determined, still pushed on toward their destinations.

Mrs Rose Rich, who had been stranded at London Bridge Station since just after 6 p.m. was finally allowed to cross over to

Monument Underground Station. When she reached the North Bank, Mrs Rich and her anonymous gentleman companion unceremoniously parted company. She never found out his name or if he ever made it to St Mary's Underground Station, which had been closed for a few years and was damaged by bombs on this night. From the Monument Station, Mrs Rich's journey home to Plaistow was normal and uninterrupted. When she arrived at her house, Mrs Rich collapsed from exhaustion on her doorstep.

Fire-fighting units still were arriving in the City, Islington, and Southwark from within the Greater London Region and throughout the home counties, as they had been for over an hour. They were too late to do anything about most of the damage, but at least they would have some water to help them keep the flames at bay.

The tide was finally coming in. Water was now being relayed from the Thames, via three and one half inch fire hose, into the 5,000-gallon dams throughout the district. It was only a trickle, really, but a very crucial trickle. A few hours earlier and it might have made all the difference.

At the heart of the inferno, however, the cataracts of the Nile would have been useless. The incoming tide was no help to anyone on Fore Street, where Auxiliary Fireman E. Geoffrey Mosely and his fellows were fighting a losing battle against the flames. Fore Street's entire length was a continuous twin row of blazing buildings, the same, if not worse, as when Commander Aylmer Firebrace walked through from Redcross Street Station over an hour before.

Auxiliary Fireman Mosely had never been so frightened in his life. All around him buildings were disintegrating, sending ominous creaking and rattling sounds out into the street, and the air was very hot and rife with flying bits of glowing debris. One small red-hot chunk slid under his collar and lodged halfway down his back, sizzling between his shoulder blades.

When they were ordered out of Fore Street, Mosely and the rest of the crew could not leave quickly enough. All gear was packed up on the trailer pump in record time and everyone piled into the car, the elegant Humber Snipe limousine with the crank start that towed the pump and all its equipment. Within twenty seconds of their driving away, an office block collapsed into the street where they had been working.

From Fore Street, the firemen drove south, out of the oven into the broiler. They wound up in Aldermanbury, next to Guildhall, where they were stopped by a roadblock of fallen buildings. The street was too narrow for the Humber Snipe to make a U-turn, so it became necessary to unhitch the trailer pump first, and then back up the car and turn it around. At one point during this manoeuvre, the car was only a few feet away from a blazing tobacconist shop. It stayed there only for a moment or so, while it was being backed up during the three-point turn, but Auxiliary Fireman Mosely thought it took forever before the car was driven forward again. The flames from the burning shop were so intense that he expected the petrol tank to explode.

They drove out via the same route by which they had entered Aldermanbury, and were finally put to work at a stagnant water dam behind the General Post Office. After a rough start, Auxiliary Fireman Mosely and his mates now settled down to a fairly quiet time. Mosely, the pump man, kept a steady stream of Thames river water gushing into the 5,000-gallon pool, while the rest of the crew went to look for a bite to eat. They found a place nearby, an all-night café that served night workers and taxi drivers, and went in to buy some refreshments.

The firemen selected from the café's somewhat limited fare and headed for the cashier. They were about to pay for their groceries when a big, burly customer, who stood several inches taller and weighed several stone heavier than the little Italian proprietor, intervened.

'You aren't going to charge these firemen anything . . . are you?' he intoned, challenging the shop owner to give him an argument.

'Oh no. Certainly not,' the owner sheepishly replied. It was customary for shopkeepers to give firemen a free drink or a bite to eat during an air raid. In this case, the proprietor's charity was due more to a guilty conscience than generosity.

The men left with their grub, bringing Fireman Mosely an odd mix of some dry biscuits, a tin of sardines, and a container of lemonade. He thought it all tasted very good.

In the Operations Room of Fighter Command Headquarters, north-west of London in Stanmore, Middlesex, the ritual of plotting and tracking continued throughout the night. Reports from the coastal radar stations still came in with urgent regularity, and the WAAFs on duty wielded their magnet-tipped plotting rods above the huge map of Britain, moving the red 'hostile' arrows over the southern home counties. Overseeing all this activity was the Control Officer and his staff, looking down from their gallery.

The great map, which had been crowded with hostile contacts all night, was no less congested at 11 p.m. A swarm of red arrows still pointed northward from the Channel, right at London. As far as anyone could tell, the attack, which had been going on for five hours, might well last another five.

News from the radar stations offered some hope. The tall masts at Rye, Pevensey, and Ventnor had not picked up any take-offs from the Luftwaffe bases on the Continent for an hour or so. The screens continued to register many hostiles on their way toward the English coast, however, bombers that had been airborne since before 10 p.m. Also, a steady stream of aircraft were being tracked back to their home bases in northern France. As they dipped below radar range toward their runways, the bombers disappeared from the radar scopes as if by magic.

No one at Stanmore breathed any sign of relief. The enemy raiders may not have been taking off for London at that precise moment, but this did not mean that they would not be back later. The enemy had done this in the past — sending one wave of aircraft, then following up the attack a few hours later. This break in the Luftwaffe's activity could be the end of the air raid, or might just be a lull between strikes. Nobody in the Controller's gallery was sure of anything. Everyone remained at his station.

Of the 183 bomb incidents that came through Guildhall's telephones, 29 dealt with high-explosive bombs. Most of these big bombs came down over in the eastern part of the City. A stick of five landed between Tower Hill and the Monument, knocking out a gas main. Two HEs hit The Tower itself, inflicting damage on William the Conquerer's 853 year-old White Tower.

One bomb narrowly missed American writer Polly Peabody. Miss Peabody, a friend of Assistant Divisional Officer Kenneth N. Hoare of the London Fire Brigade, was out covering tonight's attack to gather material for a still-in-the-writing book, keeping her eyes open for stories that would give the security-conscious censors fits of apoplexy. She had ridden into the fire zone with Divisional Officer Hoare. But when the car reached the vicinity of the Monument, Mr Hoare and Miss Peabody — Hoare had coined the nickname 'America' for his young protégé — went their separate ways. He had his own work to do and she had a story to cover.

The two split up and began walking in opposite directions. Neither had gone very far when a bomb came down between them, apparently much closer to Miss Peabody. The concussion picked her up and hurled her through the air, setting her down some distance away from where she had been standing.

She thought she was dead. She could not hear or see anything. After lying still for a few moments, Miss Peabody realised that the blast had thrown her underneath a fire engine, although she never could figure out how she came to land there. When her ears stopped ringing, the first thing she heard was Kenneth Hoare's distressed voice shouting, 'America! America! Are you all right?'

Polly Peabody extracted herself from beneath the fire appliance and began running toward the voice. She did not think of the bomb crater up ahead, and could not see it in the shadowy after-glow; running at full speed, she fell headlong into it. A moment later, Kenneth Hoare joined her in the crater, landing pell-mell on top of her.

Besides the high-explosive and incendiary bombs, the raiders also dropped a handful of huge, ungainly-looking objects called land mines. These land mines were actually anti-shipping mines, great eight-foot long hulks that contained nearly a ton of explosives, capable of tearing out the bowels of a warship or merchant vessel.

Nearly everything about them was sinister and unusual. Specially modified Heinkel He111s of Kampfgeschwader 4, which had been 'borrowed' from Luftflotte 2 for tonight's mission, released the land mines over the target. They descended slowly by parachute, coming down so quietly that they sometimes went unnoticed until daybreak. Several types of fuse were imbedded in these pear-shaped mammoths, any one of which might trigger its explosive core. The most diabolic was the magnetic fuse, which would be activated by the presence of any metallic object, even if an ambulance or fire engine passed within a block's distance.

When one of these mines went off on dry land, the concussion from its bursting 1,500 pounds-plus of explosives was devastating. Because the parachute allowed it to rest right on the surface of the earth, instead of punching into the ground like a falling 550-pound bomb, the shock waves from the blast cut down everything within reach. An exploding land mine could knock out an entire row of suburban houses, or level the better part of a city block, and still have enough punch left over to shatter windows two or three blocks away.

Tonight, a land mine became entangled in the signals outside Charing Cross Station, where it hung, swaying ominously in the high wind by its parachute shrouds, a few feet above a line of burning railway cars. The mere presence of a near ton of explosives constituted an emergency. Now, the situation was nearing the panic stage. The blazing cars threatened to light the thing off and destroy one of London's main rail centres, along with every living person in the area.

A crew of three firemen and one Fire Brigade officer were keeping the vicinity hosed down, pouring water into the burning railway carriages and cooling down the hanging monster. They knew nothing of the mine's trigger device, however, and could only keep their fingers crossed.

The real experts on these objects were the navy — the things were, after all, sea mines — and so a navy squad was called in to deal with the problem. The sailors arrived from Portsmouth in the early morning hours and very carefully set to work defusing the mine. It was made safe in time for Monday morning rush hour, to everyone's immense relief.

The Fire Brigade was also frantically pouring water into Guild-hall, and had been since 11 p.m. when water relays from the Thames began filling the local emergency dams. But by then it was much too late. The flames had already eaten away a large part of the building and had not yet finished their work. The sight of the firemen spraying the inferno with their puny jets of water reminded one onlooker of a group of teen-age boys spitting into a blast furnace.

The official order to evacuate Guildhall had already been issued. The City of London's ARP officer, John W. Murphy, recalls that he ordered his staff to leave the building at about midnight, although Guildhall records show that the order came after 11 p.m. At any rate, the ARP staff was led across Gresham Street to the City of London Police Headquarters in the Old Jewry, which was south of the fire zone and not endangered by the north-easterly wind. On the way out, Murphy noticed that Guildhall, its roof burnt away, was 'open to the sky'.

While the Fire Brigade was busy hosing down the land mine outside Charing Cross Station, a call came through to report that Number 5 Creed Lane had been hit by an incendiary. This was no more unusual than the other calls that had jammed the exchange lines for the past five and one half hours, except that it was the last one for the night. The time was 11.40.

# CHAPTER TEN

# 'The Juiciest Target in History'
## *11.40pm – 7am*

Only the toneless voices of the WAAF plotters broke the silence. The atmosphere inside the Operations Room at Fighter Command Headquarters remained as tensely quiet as it had been for the past six hours. The blue uniformed women mechanically repeated the height and range of the enemy bombers and plotted their movements — now steadily southward — on the huge table map.

From their overhead gallery, the Operations staff watched the red metal arrows retreat toward the south: across Surrey and Kent and Sussex to the Channel. Finally, the arrows were removed from the board, one by one, as the enemy crossed the Channel and arrived over the Continent.

For the first time since shortly after 6 p.m. the dark mass on the map that represented London was free from the persistent red markers. The Luftwaffe might be back later, but for now the sky over London was clear of enemy aircraft.

No one in London, not even those within the Luftwaffe's target area, had any idea that the air raid had ended. The anti-aircraft guns were now silent, but there had been lulls in the shooting throughout the attack. In the shelters, nobody was aware of anything that happened outside; they only knew what people told them. But so many stories and rumours were circulating that it was hard to know what to believe.

The firemen and roof-spotters, who had been out in it all along, were no better informed. They were surrounded by their own world of noise and flame — the fires themselves roared like a ground-borne thunderhead, and over 2,000 fire pumps rumbled out their own throb-throbbing chorus. Many hadn't heard the bombers for hours, so they could not have known that the planes were gone.

Ten minutes after the last reported bomb incident, at 11.50, the All Clear sounded. All over London, the high-pitched howl of the sirens flooded the blacked-out streets, ringing in the cars of firemen and civilians, even penetrating the interiors of air raid shelters. The local sirens certainly roused the inmates of the public shelter on Wenlock Road, Islington. M.S. Saunders heard the All Clear and breathed a sigh of relief.

There were a few who could not bring themselves to believe that it was all over. As soon as the aircraft engines and blasting anti-aircraft guns stopped, Auxiliary Fireman G.R. Hagon, fighting fires in a cobbled courtyard off Bermondsey Street in Southwark, knew that London was really in for it. Hagon thought, correctly, that the fires would be visible from as far away as the coast, and was sure that the bombers had not called it a night: ' . . . a ten year old would realise that the Luftwaffe had set us up, and would be back in a couple of hours with all the HE he could carry'.

Then the sirens started up; Hagon's heart hit his stomach.

I immediately thought the authorities were sounding an un-precedented second alert, in a desperate attempt to warn us of some new menace. I frantically tried to think what it could be – we already had rattles for gas and church bells for invasion.

When the sirens held their high note and sounded the All Clear, Hagon was 'utterly incredulous'.

The crazy thought even crossed my mind that Fifth Columnists had somehow managed to give a false All Clear. It was simply unbelievable that the Germans would miss the juiciest target in history – and how could our people be so sure that they were not coming back?

Fireman Leslie Williams, in Whitecross Street, was not alarmed, only puzzled: he could not figure out why the raid had ended so early. Charles Devall, in Morden, Surrey, wondered if the Germans were short of petrol. Then a more sinister thought occurred to him – they might be conserving their supplies for the invasion of England.

Everyone who was not sleeping heard the sirens, and many emerged from their shelters to have a look at the fires they had only heard about up to now. Some came simply out of curiosity; others left the confines of their shelters for more urgent reasons.

After five and a half hours, the sudden vacuum of silence was eerie and frightening. The long stillness created by the lifting of the anti-aircraft barrage was as bothersome as the incessant bang-banging had been. Added to this was the knowledge that it was all over, which made the shelters seem almost tomb-like. The dead quiet gave Mrs Ivy Ing a case of nervous anxiety in her basement shelter at Number 38 Lime Street. She endured it for a while, but after about an hour she could not stand it any longer and had to come up.

Usually, it was a combination of inquisitiveness along with the jitters that brought people out. When Doreen Jarvis came up for a look at the corner of Old Broad Street and London Wall, she was struck by the brightness of the fires — she doesn't remember any smoke at all, only flames and more flames, with the image of a fireman on a ladder darkly stamped upon the red backdrop. It was the heat of the fires that impressed Olive Bayliss when she and her family emerged from their London Wall shelter. She could not get over how hot the air was. The family stayed out on the street for quite some time, looking westward toward the great wind-tossed colonnades of flame. Olive's mother remarked with relief, 'They haven't got St Paul's.'

St Paul's was indeed still standing, as thousands of Londoners could verify. For some, the Cathedral was a symbol of hope, as endurable as London itself. Many who caught sight of 'Paul's' in the midst of the flames were moved and inspired by the way the old church 'took it'. But there were countless others, in Bethnal Green and Chelsea and Vauxhall and scattered areas for miles around, who wondered how long it could continue taking it.

To those who were close-up, the Cathedral's dome seemed to float on an ocean of flame. Whenever the wind shifted, the giant hemisphere changed colour, from orange to yellow to red; sometimes it was completely hidden by the flames and smoke. Few of the onlookers who gathered on Ludgate Hill to watch this bizarre scene talked to one another. When words were exchanged, they were spoken in whispers.

The few people who were still travelling through London were spared such sights, Nurse Marjorie Thyer's long walk with her anonymous gentleman companion finally ended when she reached an Underground station. After the long and cheerless journey, the reigning peace and tranquillity within the station came as something of a surprise. Shelterers were spread out all over the platform, eating, sleeping, playing cards, and carrying on as though nothing at all were happening outside. Nurse Thyer was astonished at their unconcern with 'the inferno only a few feet above them'.

It was here that Nurse Thyer said good-bye to her friend and went off on her own. She started off toward University College Hospital, where she was due back on duty, while he headed for his own destination. The two of them had walked all the way from New Cross Station through the air raid, and neither knew the other's name.

Now that the fire raid had ended, the tally of bomb damage was complete. Feldmarschall Hugo Sperrle's strategy had been totally successful. The toy-like incendiary bombs laid waste to roughly one and one-half square miles of London. Transportation was thrown into a turmoil and communications, with the rest of Britain as well as overseas, had been sharply disrupted.

The Wood Street Telephone Exchange and the General Post Office Telephones were burnt out. Four railway stations had been shut down. Five bridges across the Thames, as well as all roads in and around the City, were blocked to traffic. Gas mains and water mains were knocked out. Well-known business firms, producing goods for Britain's war effort, had been destroyed. And although the attack had ended, the flames within the target area still burned brilliantly, leaving London wide open to a follow-up strike.

The 'Raiders Past' sirens made little difference to the firemen on duty. It would still be many hours before their night would come to an end.

Most units at work within Feldmarschall Sperrle's target zone at least had an adequate supply of water at their disposal. Relays from the Thames were now bringing in a steady, if small, supply, and hoses that had been flat and limp all night were finally charged with constant pressure. But the water had come hours too late. Seemingly unstoppable, the flames continued to spread with the south west wind.

Auxiliary Fireman James Mayes' pump had been at a fire on Aldersgate Street for several hours, and was running low on fuel. Mayes had gone out in search of the fuel wagon, which was supposed to have been a quarter of a mile away on Chiswell Street, but when he went there, he was told that the tanker had left the area. After a futile trip, Mayes had no choice but to return empty-handed to Aldersgate Street and report what had happened.

On his way back, Auxiliary Fireman Mayes had an unnerving brush with terror, the inbred terror that man has for fire, an instinct that goes deeper than any fireman's training. Because of the smoke and billowing flame in the Barbican area, Mayes was having trouble seeing, so he stopped at a crossroads to get his bearings. But instead of calming him, this brief pause triggered a scalp-tingling fright. As he looked around, he could not see another living person. There were only flames raging all around him, in every direction. He was on the verge of panic when a gust of wind shifted the blaze, allowing Mayes to catch a glimpse of some firemen working over on the Barbican. After taking a long, hard look, Mayes ran straight toward them.

Actually, Auxiliary Fireman Mayes was lucky to have escaped so easily. Hundreds of firemen had been injured so far, badly enough to be taken to hospital. Over one hundred had been taken to St Bartholomew's Hospital alone. Twelve firemen had been killed, burned to death or buried by falling walls. Of these twelve, eight had been members of the wartime Auxiliary Fire Service.

There had been no casualties as a result of the Guildhall fire, which was only just short of a miracle. Most of the volunteers who had stayed inside Guildhall, salvaging centuries-old records and artefacts, now began straggling over to the public shelter at Number 8 Basinghall Street. Inside the shelter, the men found several mattresses but no blankets. It was just as well, since nobody felt much like sleeping, anyway. They sat and talked, uncoiling pent-up nerves by rehashing their experiences of the long, frustrating night. The most frequent topics were the tightly locked Church of St Lawrence Jewry and the failed water pressure.

Several of the Guildhall crew went out to look for a cup of tea, and a sandwich. While they were walking through the district, Fireguard R.C.M. Fitzhugh noticed that it was beginning to rain.

Feldmarschall Hugo Sperrle realised that he had no other choice. It had been raining for several hours in Paris, and there was no let-up in sight. Almost every one of Luftflotte 3's airfields had reported that they were socked-in; many runways were unusable, choked with mud. From his suite in the Hotel Luxembourg, on Paris' Left Bank, Feldmarschall Sperrle finally cancelled the second attack.

It had been a reluctant decision, and it had taken Sperrle several hours to arrive at it. The first strike had plastered the target with incendiaries, and London was ripe for a second strike. But he could not order another attack in this filthy weather. One bomber, a Ju88 of KG51, had already crashed while trying to land at Orly field. If Sperrle went ahead with his original plan, he would certainly lose many more aircraft and crews.

No use brooding about it; there was nothing he could do about the weather. Feldmarschall Sperrle issued his instructions to his staff officers, who began relaying the orders by telephone. With this done, there was nothing else that could be accomplished tonight, so Sperrle went to bed.

The second wave, as Feldmarschall Sperrle had outlined it, would have obliterated the City. Luftflotte 3's bomb aimers could not have failed to put hundreds of tons of high-explosive bombs dead on the brightly lit target, smashing what had not already been set afire. Remaining telephone exchanges, such as the Faraday Building's phone links, would have been blasted apart, along with the district's railway stations. Every historic building and shrine, including St Paul's Cathedral and probably all of the Wren churches, would lie in heaps of rubble next to the military objectives. The City of London would have ceased to exist.

Feldmarschall Sperrle's order to stand down was not met with any wild cheering throughout northern France. It had been apparent for some time that there would be no more take-offs tonight. Sperrle's cancellation order was only a confirmation. When the official communiqué clicked through the teletype, every-one trudged off toward their huts and, like their Feldmarschall, went to bed.

*

"A damaging blow had been dealt to the business and commerce center of London."
Farringdon Street in the City. This area suffered only "moderate" damage in the fire raid.
Some blocks in the City were completely leveled.

It seemed an eternity since the sirens had wailed their spine-chilling chorus, and it was beginning to look as if the night would never end. On both sides of the Thames, the fires were still out of control — but were no longer spreading as quickly as before. The link-ups from the river to the empty 5,000 gallon emergency water dams were finally having some effect; the water had allowed the members of the many fire services to begin holding the flames back.

Dirty, haggard, and overwhelmingly fatigued, the firemen had no idea what they were accomplishing. Some had been in the fire zone for eight straight hours, and were so desperately tired that it was an effort just to keep their eyes open.

For Fireman L.P. Andrews and the crew of his fireboat, who were now pumping Thames river water into the burning City, it had been quite a job just to reach their station. Fireman Andrews had arrived at Tower Pier, about 300 yards west of Tower Bridge, from Tilbury, Essex at about 2.30 a.m. Because of the river's low tide, it had taken him all night to travel the twenty-odd miles upstream.

Sometimes, just one welcome incident would be enough to take the edge off the long, gruelling night. In an alleyway near St Bride's Church, which was now thoroughly eaten away by flame, a pub owner risked her licence by opening at 2 a.m. Fireman A. Rosefield and his mate were 'regaled with free beer'. After they had stood in the hot, smoke-filled courtyard for several hours, the drinks went down very nicely.

Sub-Officer Sid Willmott missed out on the canteen van when he was ordered out of the Barbican and sent east to Woolwich. By 2.30 or so, his crew was feeling tired, dejected, and very hungry. Sometime during the early morning hours, an elderly lady walked up to Sub-Officer Willmott, placed a carrier bag in his hands and asked, 'Would the firemen like a sandwich?'

They were real navvy sandwiches, great hunks of bread with slabs of turkey inside. The crew quickly devoured them and took turns popping into a local pub, which was strictly illegal for the firemen and the pub owner. But this publican also turned a blind eye to the rules and regulations. Willmott remarked that he and his men would have become 'well and truly plastered' if they had drunk all the free beer offered to them.

For most of the crews there was no respite, only hour upon hour of holding a pressurised branch in sweltering heat and stinging smoke. Not many were inclined to notice that the night sky was giving way to daybreak. By 5.30 the sun was up but, because of the drizzle and overcast sky, was hidden from view. All that was visible were clouds. Dismal grey rain clouds lowered over the scarred city. More striking were the dark and ugly clouds of smoke, which stretched for miles over London, fouling the air with their stale sour smell.

But the relays from the Thames were now having their full effect, and the crews of more than two thousand fire engines were finally able to do something more than stand idly by while the City and Southwark burned all around them. Slowly and painfully, the battle of the flames was being turned. By 7.30, the fires north and south of the river were contained, and no longer spreading.

# CHAPTER ELEVEN

# 'My God, that's a Bright Sunrise'
## *7am – 9am*

When Mrs G. White opened the front door of her parents' house in Upminster, Essex, to get the milk, she found the porch covered by a thick layer of burnt paper. The sight of the charred bits came as something of a surprise; she couldn't understand where they had come from. Her first thought was that they were ashes from a bonfire, but that couldn't be, not in the blackout. Mrs White picked up some of the rubbish and saw at once that they were burnt pieces of office ledgers – and the only place where that many account books were kept was the City of London.

Most people were not taken as completely by surprise. The noise of the bombers and the pounding of the anti-aircraft last night had been plain enough, and the still raging fires were clearly visible for miles in the early Monday morning mist.

But air raid or not, another working day was about to begin. In another hour or so, shops and business firms and offices within the City and throughout London, or at least the ones that were still standing, would be re-opening.

It is man's nature to resist change. After every calamity throughout the history of the world, people have always tried to go ahead with their daily lives as normally as possible. This has nothing to do with anything as dramatic as bravery or heroism, but is merely instinct. During the September through November air raids, when the Luftwaffe bombed London for fifty-seven consecutive nights, the morning after each attack saw workers making their way around bomb damage to their jobs, and housewives trying their luck in the local shops. This morning, after the great fire raid, was no different.

Past experience taught London workers that the morning after an air raid always meant chaotic traffic problems, and that it was wise to leave for work much earlier than usual. Today, even an early start was not much of a help. Every road and all four bridges into the ravaged City district were closed to automobiles, and travelling conditions elsewhere in Central London were far from normal. The Victoria Embankment was one of the closed down avenues. Its entire length was blocked, because of bomb craters and the unexploded land mine caught up in the signals outside Charing Cross Station. London Transport issued an official report on the travel situation, beginning with this comically understated appraisal: 'As a result of the intense attack last night, traffic conditions in the Central London area are bad.'[1]

Travelling by train was not much of an improvement. All but one of the railway stations in the City and Southwark were closed. The only station still operating was Liverpool Street Station. But even these trains ran late. The official notice that greeted passengers read: 'Due To Enemy Action Trains Will Be Subject To Delay.'

Mrs D. Bugden caught the 7.42 a.m. train into Liverpool Street Station. Everyone in Mrs Bugden's compartment sat and looked idly out of the window, not saying a word to one another, just like on every other morning. As the train neared the City, the passengers caught their first glimpse of the sight up ahead. The whole skyline was vividly alight, the redness reflected by the low-hanging overcast. An air of foreboding took hold of the riders. Suddenly, one man stood up and cried out, 'My God, that's a bright sunrise!' The man sitting opposite answered, to no one in particular, 'That's no sunrise, that's a fire.' No one in the compartment said very much afterward, as everyone's eyes focussed on the startling brightness that came steadily toward them.

Most people who worked in or near the City rode their usual trains or buses as far as they would go, and then walked the rest of the way. Many walked for a mile or more, over heaps of bricks and rubble and leaking fire hoses, arriving at their jobs wet and grimy. Clerks and shorthand typists often showed up hours late, and were congratulated for having showed up at all.

Each person who entered the fire zone caught his own personal vignette of the scene. All alike and all very different, depending upon where the eye first fell.

[1] Charles Graves, *London Transport Carried On.*

For A.Y. Jessiman, there was the criss-cross of fire hose on Ludgate Hill, which looked like a snake pit. For H.T. Freeman, there were the flames jetting out of a damaged gas main next to a No Smoking sign. T.R. Tower was struck by the undamaged pubs amid the burnt-out buildings on New Bridge Street. The Blackfriars, The Albion, and The King Lud on Ludgate Circus all were still there, 'pearls among the ruins'.

After they made their way around roadblocks and through police lines, thousands arrived at work only to find that their offices or factories had disappeared during the night. Hundreds of firms had been destroyed, irreparably disrupting countless lives, wiping out businesses that had taken a lifetime to build up. Many of the displaced workers simply wandered aimlessly about, not knowing what else to do. A crowd had gathered outside St Paul's as though hoping that some of the Cathedral's charm might rub off on them.

Most waited about for their bosses to arrive and tell them what to do, just like always. Sometimes, the employers and managers were in a more confused state of mind than their workers. Mrs Evelyn Wright was informed by a policeman that her company, Ryland's Wholesale Warehouse in Wood Street, had been ruined by fire, and that her boss was waiting at an address in St Paul's Churchyard to pay off the staff. Mrs Wright found her employer sitting outside at an improvised desk, visably distraught and in tears. He handed her a pay packet and wished her the very best of luck.

Fifteen year-old Dorothy Harms, who was to start her first day of work this morning, did nto even fare as well as that. Carrying sandwiches from home, Dorothy and her school pal, Florrie, reached their factory and discovered a smouldering, blackened wreck. She had lost her first job before she had a chance to start it.

A damaging blow had been dealt to the business and commerce centre of London. Although censorship would try to keep damage to war-related industry a secret — newspapers would emphasise historic buildings and churches that had been destroyed — employees of firms within the fire zone could see much of the damage for themselves.

'Row upon row of blackened shells and free-standing walls . . .' Three City workers survey the damage along London Wall. The condition of the roadway is typical of what people had to stumble over on their way to work.

Some of it could be quickly repaired. Fenchurch Street Station, put out of action because of damaged signals and rubble-clogged tracks, was overhauled and back in operation within hours. But most of the damage would not be put right for quite some time. Many places stayed closed for several days to sort out records, and rail traffic was in a complete turmoil until after New Year.

Much of it could never be mended. Entire warehouses, filled with food and supplies, had gone in the flames, along with the offices that dispatched the provisions and the factories that produced or processed them.

Probably the most disrupted of the 'essential war services' was the communications network. Telephone and Telegraph cables, and also their nerve centres, were knocked out. The Post Office telephones on King Edward Street were a total loss — the building itself had been burned out, and the basement, with all its transformers, was flooded. Strangely, the neighbouring wings of the General Post Office were hardly damaged at all.

Also destroyed was the Central Exchange on Wood Street, as was every other building on both sides of the road. Telephonist D.N. Chambers and eleven co-workers from the Central Exchange were sent out to open an information bureau on Cheapside, to help ease the loss of communications by helping bomb-damaged firms to contact their clients. Engineers even rigged emergency telephones. But this was no help at all since the telephone lines were out.

Feldmarschall Hugo Sperrle was thoroughly disappointed. It was no one's fault that his second strike had been called off last night. The heavy weather was just bad luck. But to give up an opportunity like the one he had, to have set the heart of London vividly ablaze and not be able to follow up the attack, gnawed away at his martial sensibilities.

Sperrle had no real idea of the extent of damage that his bombers had inflicted. Reports from bomber crews constantly mentioned *sehr starke Brände*, 'fierce fires', in the target area, but these were too vague to be of any value. And it would be impossible for reconnaissance planes to photograph the target, since London was still covered by dense cloud layers. As far as the

Feldmarschall was concerned, only half of an air raid had been launched.

An official report filed a few days later illustrates the Luftwaffe's lack of detailed information. 'Toward the end of the attack,' the document declares, 'there were over one hundred widely spread fires with dense, black clouds of smoke, mainly in the City and to the north.' Actually, more than 1,500 combustions resulted from the fire bombs alone, with more flames brewing up with the help of the strong wind. Such an understatement is excusable when the limited visibility over the target is taken into account.

The men who flew the Heinkels and Junkers apparently had a much higher evaluation of their bombing mission than Feldmarschall Sperrle however. More than just a hint of gloating emerges when the air raid is summed up in the official Luftwaffe report: 'Rarely ever were fires of such number and size perceived during a single attack against the capital.'

Sperrle's opinion was shared by the rest of the Luftwaffe's general staff, as well as by the Nazi Ministry of Propaganda. If Dr Josef Goebbels, the head of the Propaganda Ministry, had got wind of the chaos created by last night's raid, he would have issued one of his usual, graphic and long-winded descriptions of the attack over the air waves. Goebbels was never given to understatement; air attacks on British cities were always proudly broadcast as victories by the Luftwaffe. After the attack on Coventry, Goebbels even coined the phrase *coventrised*, meaning 'razed to the ground'. But on the 30th, only this routine communique was issued: 'Strong bomber formations attacked London again last night.'

Within the next few days, Intelligence would learn the full effects of the bombing of 29th December. Then, the propagandists would jump into high gear, gloating over the fire damage and boasting that 100,000 incendiaries had been dropped. (Actually, about 24,000 fell.)

For now, however, they did not even bother with the usual practice of interviewing bomber crews. Because half of the mission had been cancelled, the raid was not considered important enough to warrant it.

The Luftwaffe High Command was not the only group that was at a loss. In London, people who worked right in last night's target zone were not aware of all the damage, even though there was wreckage all around. Many of the fires that were thought to have been extinguished were smouldering secretly in basements or under heaps of rubble. From time to time these smoulderings would burst into life, threatening any occupied buildings nearby.

On Bouverie Street, two office blocks which were thought to be safe suddenly erupted with flame, forcing the occupants of neighbouring buildings to evacuate. When Mrs D. Collings arrived at work in the modern Faraday Building, she found everything totally disorganised. There was no heat and no hot water, and the telephone lines to the Continent were down. To make matters worse, she and the other employees were warned that the building might have to be abandoned. Firemen were still 'damping down' the charred hulks surrounding the Faraday Building, and nobody knew if these bombed-out places were secure.

In buildings that had been only slightly damaged or had escaped entirely, workers did their best to get on with their jobs. Only it was not easy. Electricity was off, and before the day was out candles had to be rationed. Overcoats and gloves had to be worn indoors to protect against the numbing cold. And always there was the smoke and fine chalk dust and the unique smell of burnt wet wood that stung the nostrils.

Firms that still had offices co-operated with 'orphans' in the same line of work. Mrs B.E. Smith's employer, a solicitor, shared his King Street office with an elderly lawyer until the old gentleman's safe could be opened — the flames had welded it shut. When the safe finally was opened by the Civil Defence Rescue Squad, whose knowledge of acetyline equipment made them heir to this unlikely task, only ashes remained inside. The intense heat had turned the strongbox into an incinerator. It would take years to sort out all the wills and documents that had been lost.

Reactions were not always predictable. Sometimes one man's anguish was another man's joy. Ernest Boyd's firm, Simpkin and Marshall's wholesale booksellers in Ave Maria Lane, was all but totally destroyed, but Mr Boyd was not in the least bit sorry. Although he had worked there for several years, he cordially hated the place. While watching flames consume what was left of the building, Boyd made a mental comparison between one of his superiors, who had bullied and harassed and made life unpleasant for him ever since he joined the company, and Adolf Hitler: 'One tyrant destroying another.'

After a while, the company's manager wandered by, talking distractedly to himself. Nearly overcome by worry and distress, the man heaved glance after baleful glance at the smouldering ruin and asked no one in particular what he was going to do. Ernest Boyd heard him and blithely replied, 'I don't know about you, but I'm going down to my Union Hall and get another job.' The manager was shocked by what he considered to be Boyd's 'indecent flippancy'.

On the morning after every air raid, cleaning up seemed to take priority over all else. Any company or block of flats that could still open its doors began tidying up almost as soon as the working day began. The first task was usually sweeping up the blasted-out window glass from the pavement. For many Londoners, the sound of broken glass shards being swept into dustbins is a unique noise, disquieting even after years of peacetime. It is a sound inexorably linked with the war, a reminder of the impermanence of life and of the winter when the Luftwaffe brought the battlefield to their own streets and houses.

For although the damage done by last night's bombing was largely industrial, not every building was a factory or warehouse. On Goswell Road and Golden Lane and Farringdon Road and on many other streets on both sides of the Thames, hundreds of flats were destroyed by fire, leaving whole families homeless. Southern Islington lost the largest number of dwellings and also suffered the highest rate of civilian casualties. Most of those killed were either crushed to death or cremated when all the floors of their blazing building caved into the basement shelter.

When Eileen Waterman and her father arrived at their block of flats in the Peabody Buildings, just north of the Barbican, they discovered a squad of firemen at work outside. After the officer in charge gave them permission to go up and have a look, the two of them climbed the stairs to their upper storey flat.

As soon as they stepped inside, it became clear that they would

not be able to live there anymore. The Watermans found everything charred and blackened. Piles of rubble as high as the gas
stove covered the floor. The roof was gone, burnt through by a
cluster of fire bombs. When Miss Waterman looked up, she could
see the leaden morning sky.

Hundreds of other families faced the same ordeal. Some lost
everything in the fire: clothes, heirlooms, all they owned in the
world. Jets from fire hoses often did as much damage as the
bombs. Basement flats and shelters were flooded out. Floors and
ceilings in upper stories caved in from water damage. Many spent
the entire day salvaging their drenched belongings.

Once in a while, a story had a happy ending.

After a night's sleep, Frank Paling resumed his search for his
wife's mother, whose block of flats on Aldersgate Street had
been burnt out. Last night, the local Air Raid Wardens informed
him that the missing party had been taken to Clerkenwell, so
Mr Paling left his home in Southwark and began walking towards
his destination, over Southwark Bridge and around the City's still
burning derelict buildings.

When he reached Clerkenwell, about a mile and a quarter north
of his home, Frank Paling began asking people in the district if
they had any clue as to his mother-in-law's whereabouts. It was a
long, drawn-out process, but it did get results. After hours of
asking about, Paling was directed to a nearby address. There, in a
'refugee flat', Paling found her. Other than being somewhat tired
and drawn, she was very much alive and none the worse for her
adventure.

# CHAPTER TWELVE

# 'Too Late, as Usual'
## *After 9am*

All of the Luftwaffe's chiefs were as dissatisfied with 29th December's *Nachteinsatz* as Feldmarschall Sperrle, and so was the Chancellor of the Third Reich, Adolf Hitler. Hitler and Reichsmarschall Hermann Göring had planned the raid in retaliation for the R A F's bombing of Berlin. Neither were happy that London had escaped so lightly. General Hans Jeschonnek, Chief of the Luftwaffe staff and proponent of 'mass panic' bombing, shared in the prevailing displeasure.

The weather reports for the next few days offered no hope for a follow-up attack. Low cloud and rain were expected to cover Britain and northern Europe for at least forty-eight hours, keeping the bomber bases closed down.

London had escaped the full measure of Adolf Hitler's wrath this time, but there would be other opportunities, and Hitler would see that each one was exploited to the fullest. The clouds would have to lift sometime, and when they did the Luftwaffe would be ready. London was too big a target, and too full of tempting landmarks and objectives, to be missed.

After the Great Fire of 1666 burned itself out, a tract of the old walled City of London measuring one and a half miles long, from the Temple to Tower Hill, by one and a half miles wide, from the Thames northward to Cripplegate, lay in ashen desolation. On this Monday morning, 30th December 1940, the fire damage was not as centralised and was more difficult to pace off in square measurements, but would remain the largest area of destruction in London throughout the Blitz, and perhaps the worst in Britain.

Three separate areas were burnt out, looking from the air like great bald splotches on the landscape. On the South Bank, a narrow strip of Southwark, roughly a mile long and a quarter mile wide at its broadest point near London Bridge Station, had been ruined by flames. Across the river an irregular region, roughly one third of a mile square, still smouldered to the north and west of the Tower.

But the bulk of the destruction was in the City's western half, extending into southern Islington. On a map, this region resembles the shape of a very rough, inverted T. Along its north-to-south 'downstroke', major fires had raged from the Thames to Dingley Road, a mile and a quarter long stretch. The 'cross' of the upside-down T ran between Fetter Lane and Cannon Street Railway Station, about a mile in length.

In the centre of this region lay what had been the core of last night's inferno, now the scene of the worst of the fire damage. This includes the Barbican—Moorgate area, the entire vicinity around Guildhall, and the surrounding environs of St Paul's Cathedral. Almost every building within this district had been destroyed. Row upon row of blackened shells and free-standing walls swayed and creaked in the wind. The entire length of Wood Street and Fore Street were in ruins. North of St Paul's Cathedral in Paternoster Row, twenty-seven publishing firms and their warehouses and five million books had gone up in a brilliant, colossal bonfire.

In the Barbican vicinity, nothing but charred remains stood except for the partially burnt-out Whitbread's Brewery, the Cripplegate Institute, and, the height of irony, Redcross Street Fire Station. Every other structure in the district — St Giles Cripplegate Church, just across the road from the fire station; all the buildings and warehouses on Jewin Street and Redcross Street — was now a calcined, fire-blackened ruin. The firehouse itself, although a bit charred, would remain in service. On the land made vacant by the flames, after the Royal Engineers had pulled down all the unsafe hulks, the firemen and firewomen attached to Redcross Street Station would raise a thriving flower and vegetable garden, even planting apple trees.

Besides the blocks of flats and transportation links and war-related manufacturing centres, many relics of the City of London's rich and vivid history also had perished. Thirteen churches designed by Christopher Wren were either completely ruined or severely damaged. Four churches that had survived the Great Fire of 1666 also were victims of the air raid, including All Hallows by-The-Tower, where Samuel Pepys had watched the 1666 Fire from the steeple. Brewer's Hall and Barber's Hall, two of the City's historic company halls, had burned. Dr Samuel Johnson's house in Gough Square also suffered fire damage, but the destruction had been confined to the top floor and was eventually repaired.

The immediate blame for the Great Fire of 1666 fell upon the Lord Mayor, Sir Thomas Bludworth, who had gone back to bed after being told of the outbreak of fire. In the wake of the fire blitz and the extensive damage wrought by the small, easily extinguishable two pound incendiary bombs, a similar wave of anger erupted from every borough in Greater London. This anger was directed not so much at the Luftwaffe as at the landlords and company managers who failed to post roof spotters at their buildings. Outraged letters to newspaper editors and entries in wartime diaries suggest that charges of criminal negligence be brought against these imprudent firms and their directors. Harsher critics simply ranted and hurled epithets, declaring that the fires were every bit as much the fault of City landlords as the enemy bombers.

A very small minority took an altogether different view. Architects and urban planners almost rejoiced over the loss of the City's old fire trap office blocks. In the periodical *London Calling*, commentator McDonald Hastings wrote:

> If . . . Wren's most beautiful churches and some of the City's most noble and historic buildings are damaged irreparably, they have taken with them in their passing some of the dreariest and meanest stretches of Victorian office buildings in the whole of the City of London . . . The Hun is giving us a priceless opportunity to re-conceive the City on a more rational and liveable plan.

American writer Beatrice L. Warde added that it would have taken twenty-five years to accomplish as much needed demolition, and goes on to say that the Wren churches can be rebuilt in facsimile, if anyone wants them.

This may not have been the most widely held opinion, but it certainly was far-sighted. The face of the district would eventually feel the full impact of modernisation, probably more than any other London region. Whole streets — Redcross Street; Jewin Street; Dowgate Dock; and a score of small avenues and alleys — would disappear from the map to make way for new construction. The direction of the western half of London Wall would be changed, and many other roadways would be altered. Of the seventeen ruined City churches, only eight would be rebuilt. Blocks of concrete and steel and glass would replace the tightly-packed Victorian and Edwardian buildings. For better or worse, the City of London would never be the same after 29th December 1940.

The outcry over roof spotters produced immediate results. On Tuesday the 31st, Herbert Morrison, the Home Secretary and Minister for Home Security, gave a speech calling for more fire watchers and volunteer firemen. Three weeks later, Morrison's Fire Precautions and Business Premises Order was officially adopted, requiring men between the ages of sixteen and sixty to register for forty-eight hours of fire watching every month.

These actions did little to mollify the public's anger. Morrison's plan was derided for having come four months behind time; the general feeling was that something should have been done last September, when the Blitz against London first began. After hearing Morrison's speech, Charles Devall of Morden, Surrey noted in his diary: 'He is too late, as usual.' And, as it turned out, the Fire Precautions Order was almost totally ineffective. The order contained so many escape clauses that three-quarters of all who registered were exempted from standing watch.

Last night, once the fires had taken hold, even fire spotters could not do very much. Guildhall's fire crew had been right on the job but, because of one piece of bad luck after another, their building had burned just the same. In the bleak Monday light, charred beams lay in a heap across the Great Hall, and the wrought iron decorative tracery, twisted by the intense heat, had been distorted into grotesque and shapeless blobs of metal. The walls themselves remained intact, although covered by a thick crust of soot and grime, allowing the hall to be rebuilt once again.

'This "square mile" was originally a walled city . . .' A section of the old Roman Wall after the air raid damage is cleared to one side.

The commander of Guildhall's Fire Squad, F.A. George, noticed that the flagpole over the main entrance had survived the night. He produced a Union Jack and ran it up to the top of the staff, 'a symbol which all the world would see and understand'.

At about 10 a.m. the Guildhall Fire Squad assembled in the public shelter at Number 8 Basinghall Street, where most of the crew had spent an uncomfortable night in wet overalls. Commander George gave everyone permission to go home, and the men began fanning out in all directions toward their houses. When Fireguard R.C.M. Fitzhugh reached his place about an hour later, he was still wearing his fire-watcher's uniform: helmet, gumboots, and grimy, sodden overalls. His Sunday clothes had gone in the fire.

A dispute was raised over the burning of Guildhall, a miniature of the controversy that surrounded the burning of the City. The fact that a single, foot-long fire bomb had destroyed both the church of St Lawrence Jewry and Guildhall seemed unbelievable to anyone who had not been there; officials threatened to charge members of Guildhall's staff with negligence, resulting in the loss of the historic hall.

The upshot of this argument was a statement by the Guildhall librarian, who stated that the keys to St Lawrence Jewry had been available all along. According to this report, a notice which gave the exact location of the keys was left by the rector of St Lawrence's and placed 'in so prominent a position that a blind man could have seen it — had he looked for it.'

The threatened charges of negligence came to nothing when it became clear that such charges were groundless. The bomb that caused all the damage had lodged itself in the church's steeple, outside the building; the small Guildhall crew had enough to do without climbing all over St Lawrence's. Also, the lack of water, along with the strong winds, was as much to blame as the bomb itself.

Firemen who were still at work in Feldmarschall Sperrle's target area were too tired to care about such controversies, or, for that matter, anything else. Some had been fighting fires for over fourteen hours, without a chance even to sit down. As the flames died down or burnt themselves out, the members of the fire services, both London Fire Brigade and the numerous provincial fire companies, were being sent home in increasing numbers.

Auxiliary Fireman James Mayes, who had almost panicked when he became temporarily lost amid the billowing flames near the Barbican, was totally exhausted. He had not eaten or drunk anything in more than twelve hours, and his throat felt like sandpaper from breathing the hot, smoky air all night. When he and his crew were driven back to Ambler Road School Fire Station in Finsbury Park, Mayes was too tired even to notice the time of day.

Sub-Officer Richard B. Horne and his crew extracted themselves from the rubble of Gough Square sometime during the late morning hours, and set out for their station in Wandsworth. Although the factories in the square had suffered fire damage, they had succeeded in saving most of Dr Samuel Johnson's house despite the fact that they had been without water for most of the night. But there was little time for congratulations. They would be back in the City to 'damp down' for three more days before anyone would have any time off.

One at a time, the trailer pumps towed by taxis or limousines, the turntable ladders, and the heavy units, all manned by bone-weary and indescribably filthy firemen, left the fire ground and headed for their stations. Sometimes there was a small surprise to hurry the departing firemen on their way. At Tower Pier, Fireman L.P. Andrews and his crew were still aboard their fire-boat and, as they had been doing since the small hours, pumping water from the Thames into the fires. During the late morning, their fireboat was approached by a naval launch.

The officer aboard the launch hailed the firemen: 'What are you doing there?'

'Pumping water,' Andrews replied.

'What time did you arrive?' the launch persisted.

'About 2.30,' Andrews answered.

'Was there anyone here when you arrived?'

'No.'

'Well, you'd better get the hell out of it. I evacuated this area at about 1.30. You are probably about twenty feet off a parachute bomb.'

The fireboat's crew stopped the pumps, disconnected the hoses, let go the ropes, and let the tide take them well clear before starting their engines for the trip back to Tilbury.

In contrast with the damage to property, loss of life was disproportionately low. 163 persons were killed, 509 injured, almost miraculous considering the scale of the attack. The London Fire Brigade's number of dead and wounded also was relatively small. Twelve firemen were killed, and 250 injured. 123 casualties were sent to St. Bartholomew's Hospital for medical attention, 'comparatively few,' according to the records, mostly for minor eye injuries. All but 49 were released after treatment. Had Feldmarschall Sperrle's second wave attacked, armed with 550 lb high explosives instead of the 2 lb incendiaries, the toll of dead and wounded would have been many times this number.

The low death toll had a precedent in the 1666 Fire. Only four people were killed in the Great Fire of London, which raged for four days and nights.

Employees who lost their jobs in last night's fires endured a wide range of fates. Some went back to work within a few days, at new premises. Hitchcock, Williams & Co., formerly at 69/70 St Paul's Churchyard, began re-organising their business from temporary offices later on Monday afternoon. Leonard Atkinson, burnt out of his Ludgate Hill Building Society, was back to work the next day, transferring the company books, papers, and furniture to an evacuated house in Wimbledon, south London.

But there were many more who never got the call, and were simply paid their wages due and dismissed. The only word R.C.H. Constable ever received from his former employers, Stapley and Smith & Co. of Fore Street, was a short note asking for the return of his company-issued fire axe.

Nurse Marjorie Thyer was back at University College Hospital, with a vivid tale of her Sunday night adventure. She regaled the other sisters with the story of her walk from New Cross Station at the height of the air raid, but they found her account hard to believe. All of them had spent the night in the Nurses' Quarters, and had seen nothing nor had any idea of the severe damage. It was not until they read reports in the newspapers that Marjorie Thyer's colleagues were convinced.

The City in 1945. The damage round St Paul's gives some idea of the Cathedral's peril from the surrounding fires.

They could not have learned a great deal from the official news summaries. Wartime security and censorship had clamped a stranglehold on the release of any specific facts. Bus driver H.A. Penny of Paddington made these comments in his diary:

> I cannot find out much about last night's fire and bomb ... the 6 p.m. news tells us [only of] the wilful firing of the City of London and severe damage.

Mrs Constance Miles of Guildford, Surrey was much more emphatic about the lack of information.

> The tame little talk on this vast, hateful fire given by Robin Duff in the BBC made us feel sick. No details; everything about the bravery of the firemen and the capital way the ARP behaved. Sickening.

The newspapers were as tight-lipped as the radio broadcasters. Monday's 'Late London' edition of *The Times* featured this two-column heading on page 4:

## FIRE BOMBS RAINED ON LONDON
## MANY BUILDINGS HIT
### Famous Wren Church Destroyed

The story beneath was as dim as the headline. Strict censorship banned editors from printing a more extensive report.

Within the week, newspapers would be allowed to run fuller accounts. Guildhall and other places — none of any military importance — would be mentioned by name. The *Daily Express* would even concoct a fanciful story about a 'night air battle' over London during the raid. But for now, wartime security slammed a tight lid on everything. No particulars were published. Better to run vague, non-informative stories than to be charged with supplying 'information of value to the enemy'.

The news media might have been reticent about the air raid, but another topic was given top priority. American president Franklin D. Roosevelt had given his latest 'fireside chat' at 9.30

A view looking north-west from the Dome of St Paul's and showing the damage caused by the enemy bombing. The photograph was taken in 1950.

Washington, DC time, pledging support to Britain and proclaiming that the United States 'must be the great arsenal of democracy'. *The Times* gave as much space to Roosevelt's speech as to last night's attack, leaving out no details. Every other paper followed suit, printing lengthy excerpts from the address. 'ROOSEVELT SAYS AMERICA MUST BE ARSENAL FOR DEMOCRACY', announced the banner headline of the *News Chronicle*.

Reaction to Roosevelt's speech was overwhelmingly favourable, but not everyone was pleased. Mrs Constance Miles once again had a few remarks:

> Roosevelt's speech came over the wireless at eight this morning, all on our side. He said that from all the inside information he had, he thought that Britain was to win this war. But will the Americans ever realise the situation as long as they don't spare any soldiers?

As the bleak, grey day went on, people in and near the fire zone paused from time to time in order to look at the desolation around them, as though they were unwilling, or unable, to take the shock all at once. After finishing her morning's work, Mrs Eileen Dale walked along Cheapside toward St Paul's. She was not moved by the sight of the Cathedral among the ruins as much as by the dozens of small, burnt-out shops, still smouldering in the afternoon overcast. St Bride's Church was also a smouldering wreck, but Jack Miles who worked for the *Evening Standard* was surprised that it was still recognisable at all. When he last saw the church it had been boiling with flame, but today its slender steeple, 'pointing straight up, as if there was nothing wrong with it,' still graced the Fleet Street skyline. There were many people who caught sight of workers tending to normal activities, such as watching a crew load a newspaper van, and thought it wonderful to see them doing their everyday jobs.

For many others, everyday affairs would take some time to put in order. New places of employment had to be found, flats had to be rented, new surroundings needed to be adopted to. Lifetimes of habits were disrupted; new ones would not be developed quickly or simply.

Eileen Waterman and her father had been among the unlucky who lost both home and living in the air raid. Their flat in Roscoe Street was roofless and filled with rubble, and Mr Waterman's firm, Dowlings and Co. of Jewin Street, had been destroyed.

Before any kind of a normal workaday routine could be worked out, the Watermans would have to find somewhere else to live. Eileen's sister had a place in Northfleet, Kent, and luckily was able to take both of them in to live with her. Another piece of good news came when Mr Waterman's company did not go out of business, but moved across the river to Tooley Street, Southwark. When things became settled, Mr Waterman began taking the train to work every day.

After a while, Eileen left her sister's home and moved in with a friend from work, in Bethnal Green, East London. Here, she was to have 'more excitement' in the months to come as the Blitz continued.

Mrs Frances Hine refused to let the bombs interfere with her children's planned holiday treat. Mrs Hine had watched last night's fires from her window in Isleworth, Middlesex, with a good deal of anxiety, but decided to make the trip into London to see the comedy-pantomime *Where the Rainbow Ends* after all. She and her two children walked from Charing Cross Railway Station to the New Theatre, noticing the twisted remains of Ron Woolaway's tramcar on the Embankment and encountering a 'particularly big' bomb crater at the bottom of St Martin's lane along the way. The audience at that afternoon's performance was understandably sparse. After the performance, Madame Conti, who had produced the show annually for many years, came out on stage to thank those who had come. She had not expected anyone at all to show up.

Most of the regulars and auxiliaries of the London Fire Brigade returned to their usual sweep-and-polish chores almost as soon as they got back to their station. Sub-Officer Sid Willmott, who, from atop his 100-foot turntable ladder in the fire-tossed Barbican, had announced, 'The whole bloody town's lit up!' was supposed to have gone off-duty at 9.00. But he had been 'stung again' for off-duty time. His fire appliance had broken down and, before it could go into the shop, had to be stripped of all its gear, a job that took hours. It would not be the last time this would happen during the Blitz.

Redcross Street Station, abandoned at the height of the fires, was soon back in operation, and its men once again took up their usual tasks. When Fireman James Goldsmith returned to the station, he began clearing and sorting his appliance's gear, in case of another call. Sometimes equipment and lengths of hose would be lost while on the job, which usually was a problem. Not today, however. There was plenty of gear lying about on the streets. Nearby Whitecross Street was littered with several burnt-out and abandoned trailer pumps, complete with tools and equipment. The hardware merely had to be picked up and carried off.

Sub-Officer Fredrick Offord, also of Redcross Street Station, walked into the firehouse carrying one of the many unexploded incendiaries scattered about the streets. One of the firemen spotted it and announced that it was 'one of our bombs'. To prove his point, the man proceeded to put the bomb in a vice, unscrew the end, and remove the combustible filler. He then located the stamp mark inside and showed it to Sub-Officer Offord. The stamp showed that the bomb had been manufactured in 1938 by an engineering company in Islington; it had apparently been sold to the German government shortly before the war broke out.

The great fire raid was over, but the sights and images of the night of 29th December would remain embedded in the minds of countless Londoners, vivid reminders of the Sunday night fires. Whenever A.G. Lewin smells smouldering timber, which, as an active member of the London Fire Brigade, he often does, the odour brings him sharply back to the City during the winter of 1940/41. A rainy day will sometimes conjure up the scent of burnt, damped-down wooden beams to American writer Polly Peabody. For years afterward, Mrs G Timbers' memory of the fire blitz was a nightmare collage of red from the burning buildings and the horrible, pallid white of the faces of shelterers at King's Cross Underground Station.

The Blitz against London was not over, however, nor would the air raids end for another four and one half months. Within two weeks, on the night of 11th January 1941, the City would once again be attacked by Feldmarschall Sperrle's bombers. One of the high-explosive bombs dropped that night would score a direct hit on the Bank Underground station, blasting bodies of those sheltering below up onto the pavement and blowing a gigantic crater in the roadway. This crater, in front of the Royal Exchange, would be so wide and deep that the Royal Engineers would have to build a bridge across it.

Between mid-January and mid-March, many small 'nuisance' raids would be flown against the capital. The next heavy raid would not come until 8th March, when the Luftwaffe would send 125 bombers to London. The raids would continue throughout March and April on a basis of roughly once a week. On the night of 19th March, 479 bombing sorties would drop over 460 tons of high explosives, killing hundreds of civilians.

The month of April 1941 would witness two great raids, remembered by Londoners as 'The Wednesday' and 'The Saturday' — 16th and 19th April — both triggered by revenge, in retaliation for RAF strikes against Berlin. 'The Wednesday' raid dropped over a thousand tons of HE and incendiaries, disrupting utilities and transportation centres and once again inflicting damage on St Paul's Cathedral. 'The Saturday' raid was slightly larger, topping off the destruction of the 16th April attack.

The last raid before Hitler would invade Russia in late June would come on the night of 10th May. To many, this was the worst of all. For six and one half hours, Feldmarschall Sperrle's Heinkels and Junkers pulverised London. When it finally ended, transportation and rail centres had been damaged and many more factories and homes were totally destroyed. Westminster Abbey, the Tower of London, the British Museum, and other famous London landmarks had been hit. Over 1,400 had been killed, and more than 1,800 injured.

Germany would not be immune from intensive bombing as the war dragged on. Just as London had suffered more than Warsaw and Rotterdam early on in the war, people living within Germany's cities would feel the full brunt of the larger and better armed Allied bombers in less than a year. Berlin would be attacked with increasing frequency and always mounting numbers. On the night of 30th May 1942, one thousand RAF bombers would raid Cologne. Right up to the end of the war, every major city within

the Third Reich — Dresden, Hamburg, Dusseldorf, Leipzig, Dort-
mund — would be bombed regularly and relentlessly, by the R A F
at night and the American Army Air Force during the day. The
Luftwaffe had learned much about strategic bombing from the
London Blitz raids, but the British and Americans also had been
learning. Auxiliary Fireman G.R. Hagon, who had been so greatly
alarmed when the sirens sounded the early All Clear in Bermondsey Street, Southwark, was stationed in Germany after the war.
Hagon got a first hand look at the terrible destruction, and was
moved to comment, 'Christ, we never knew what bombing was.'

On Monday, 30th December, however, the bombing had
stopped for the time being, allowing a semblance of life to continue in London until the next time the sirens sounded. People
living or working in the fire stricken area endured the problems
caused by last night's air raid, each in his and her own peculiar
way, and passed their day. At the end of it, everyone had somewhere to go, and had stories to tell when they got there. Some were
about lucky accidents or new beginnings; others were not so cheerful.

With the approach of darkness came the evening meal, along
with the possibility of another air raid. At about 5 p.m., Stanley
G. Champion, whose company, Jackson Brothers Ltd. of 47 Old
Street, had vanished in last night's flames, got up to have some tea
at his home in Romford, Essex. The meal passed without an interruption by the sirens. Because of the weather, still grey and overcast, it was evident by now that the bombers would not be back
tonight. Stanley Champion made this entry in his diary a short
while later: 'The night turned out to be windy with rain and I was
thankful that no warnings were sounded.'

# INDEX

# Index

AI Mk IV airborne radar, 72–3
All Hallows by-The-Tower, 197
Andrews, Fireman L.P., 184,
   201–2
Aschenbrenner, Hauptmann
   Friedrich, 41–6, 60–1, 65–6,
   71, 74, 77–8, 82–3, 87, 88,
   97, 141–2, 146
Atkinson, Leonard, 80, 92,
   130, 145, 202
Auxiliary Fire Service, 37, 63–4,
   107, 131, 181

Barbican, 33, 110, 113, 132,
   159, 181, 193, 196
Bayliss, Olive, 32, 34, 71, 79,
   179
Beaufighter (airplane), 71–73,
   74, 104–6, 121
Bell, Station Officer Thomas,
   127
Benning, L.E., 110, 137
Berlin, 26, 28, 143, 209
Blackfriars Bridge, 34, 86, 95
Blackstone, Assistant Divisional
   Officer Geoffrey, 124, 127
Blitz, The, 24, 26–8, 58–60, 68,
   72, 78, 84, 145, 186, 195,
   198, 207–8
Boyd, Ernest, 193
Britain, Battle of, 26–8, 118

Cannon Street Fire Station, 38,
   95, 116, 124–5
Cannon Street Railway Station,
   112, 122, 129, 196
Central Exchange, 34, 114,
   154, 180, 190
Chain Home Radar Stations,
   65–8, 71, 73, 171
Champion, Stanley G., 85,
   91–2, 106–7, 115, 131,
   210
Christchurch, Greyfriars, 151
Churchill, Winston, 129
Constable, R.C.H., 85–6, 140,
   160, 202
Cook, E.R., 64, 158
Coventry, 45, 55, 87, 191
Cox, Gwladys, 98, 158
Crowfoot, Special Constable
   R.E., 21, 59–60, 64, 98,
   137–8

Davis, Benjamin W., 85, 98,
   130, 157–8
Devall, Charles, 178, 198
Douglas, Air Marshal Sholto,
   66, 76, 83
Duff, Robin, 47, 204

Evelyn, John, 129